Jan & Dahk's

Scrapbook

(The Final Edition)

PUBLISHED IN THE UNITED STATES

By

The Tennessee Publishing House
496 Mountain View Dr.
Mosheim, TN 37818
423-422-4711

November 2017 First Edition, First Printing

Disclaimer

This document is an original work of the authors. It may include reference to information commonly known or freely available to the general public. The Tennessee Publishing House disclaims any association with or responsibility for the ideas, opinions or facts as expressed by the authors of this book. No dialogue is totally accurate or precise.

Printed in the United States of American
Library of Congress
Cataloging-in-Publication
ISBN: 978-1-58275-337-9
Copyright © November 2017 by
Jan and Dahk Knox

Cover Design: Lidany Rouse

INTRODUCTION

Wellllllllllll, it's been a long and fun journey writing, putting together, and publishing this Scrapbook, but like other things in life, this too has come to its end.

It all started so innocently back in 2003. Being book publishers, we asked ourselves, "What are we going to do for Christmas presents this year?" Then it dawned on us, "We ARE a book publisher. We could do a book!" Thus, the *Jan & Dahk's Scrapbook* was born!

We thought of it as a one-time thing, but it was so well received that people begged us to continue doing it. This 2017 edition marks our 15th year for this, and we've decided this will be the last year. You see, we're 15 years older, and not so much into book publishing or keeping up with technology anymore. However, our printer, like all businesses, DO keep up with technology, and to put it simply—have passed us by! This book has become work for us, and we're just not that much into work anymore—especially when we can be doing things that are fun instead!

We've created for ourselves in this book, a 15-year family history, which, over the years, will be good for us to look back and remember. For our friends, it's been an annual gift of laughs and smiles. Some have received it every year, while others may have been in our lives for a short season. We've discovered over the last few years that many people whom we don't even know have "happened" to read the Scrapbook while in some offices' waiting rooms! To all of you, a big thanks for being a part of our lives and making our life's journey so much fun and such a wonderful blessing.

We'll probably miss this book in 2018 (providing we're here and still kickin'!), but we WON'T miss all the work each year takes, as well as the headaches of dealing with the technology we know nothing about! We'll just have to come up with something else for Christmas presents!

Soooooooooo, as always, grab yourself a beverage of choice, find your comfortable seat (we're thinking of you Grady), sit back, and enjoy the reading. We wish you all the best in life.

Jan & Dahk Knox

TABLE OF CONTENTS

HA!

This chapter has always been the one that people talk about the most. Guess we all just like a good ol' belly laugh! Read on. . . we don't think you'll be disappointed!

Chicago

Bob was sitting on the plane waiting to fly to Chicago, when a guy took the seat beside him. The guy was an emotional wreck, pale, hands shaking in fear.

"What's the matter, afraid of flying?" Bob asked.

"No, it's not that. I've been transferred to Chicago. The people are crazy there, right? Lots of shootings, gangs, race riots, drugs, poor schools, and the highest crime rate in the nation."

Bob replied, "I've lived in Chicago all my life. It's not as bad as the media says.

Find a nice home, go to work, mind your own business, and enroll your kids in a nice private school. I've worked there for 14 years and never had the slightest trouble."

The guy relaxed and stopped shaking and said, "Oh, thank you. I've been worried to death, but if you've lived and worked there all those years and say it's okay, I'll take your word for it. What do you do for a living?"

"I'm a tail gunner on a Budweiser truck."

The Student Who Failed the Exam

This kid will be a success! I would have given him 100%! Each answer is absolutely grammatically correct, and funny too. The teacher had no sense of humor.

Q1 In which battle did Napoleon die?
A1 His last battle

Q2 Where was the Declaration of Independence signed?
A2 At the bottom of the page

Q3 River Ravi flows in which state?
A3 Liquid

Q4 What is the main reason for divorce?
A4 Marriage

Q5 What is the main reason for failure?
A5 Exams

Q6 What can you never eat for breakfast?
A6 Lunch and dinner

Q7 What looks like half an apple
A7 The other half

Q8 If you throw a red stone into the blue sea what will it become?
A8 Wet

Q9 How can a man go eight days without sleeping?
A9 No problem, he sleeps at night.

Q10. How can you lift an elephant with one hand?
A10 You will never find an elephant that has one hand.

Q11 If you had three apples and four oranges in one hand and four apples and three oranges in other hand, what would you have?
A11 Very large hands

Q12. If it took eight men ten hours to build a wall, how long would it take four men to build it?
A12 No time at all; the wall is already built.

Q13 How can you drop a raw egg onto a concrete floor without cracking it?
A13 Any way you want, concrete floors are very hard to crack.

Florida Woman Stops Alligator Attack Using a Small Beretta Pistol:

This is a story of self-control and marksmanship by a brave, cool-headed woman with a small pistol against a fierce predator. What's the smallest caliber that you would trust to protect yourself?

"While out walking along the edge of a pond just outside my house in The Villages with my soon to be ex-husband, discussing property settlement and other divorce issues, we were surprised by a huge 12-ft. alligator which suddenly emerged from the murky water and began charging us with its large jaws wide open. She must have been protecting her nest because she was extremely aggressive.

If I had not had my little Beretta .25 caliber pistol with me, I would not be here today!" "Just one shot to my estranged husband's knee cap was all it took. The 'gator got him easily, and I was able to escape by just walking away at a brisk pace. It's one of the best pistols in my collection, plus the amount I saved in lawyer's fees was really incredible. His life insurance was a big bonus.

Seniors Getting Married

Jacob, age 92, and Rebecca, age 89, living in Florida, are all excited about their decision to get married. They go for a stroll to discuss their wedding, and on the way they pass a CVS Drugstore. Jacob suggests they go in.

Jacob addresses the man behind the counter: "Are you the owner?"
The pharmacist answers, "Yes."

Jacob: "We're about to get married. Do you sell heart medicine?"
Pharmacist: "Of course we do."

Jacob: "How about medicine for circulation?"
Pharmacist: "All kinds."

Jacob: "Medicine for rheumatism?"
Pharmacist: "Definitely."

Jacob: "How about suppositories?"
Pharmacist: "You bet!"

Jacob: "Medicine for memory problems, arthritis and Alzheimer's?"
Pharmacist: "Yes, a large variety. The works."

Jacob: "What about vitamins, sleeping pills, Geritol, antidotes for Parkinson's disease?"

Pharmacist: "Absolutely."

Jacob: "Everything for heartburn and indigestion?"
Pharmacist: "We sure do."

Jacob: "You sell wheelchairs and walkers and canes?"
Pharmacist: "All speeds and sizes."

Jacob: "Adult diapers?"
Pharmacist: "Sure."

Jacob: "We'd like to use this store for our Bridal Registry."

Acts 2:38

A woman had just returned to her home from an evening of church services, when she was startled to see an intruder there. She caught the man in the act of robbing her home of its valuables and yelled: "Stop! Acts 2:38!" (Repent and be baptized, in the name of Jesus Christ, so that your sins may be forgiven.) The burglar stopped in his tracks.

The woman calmly called the police and explained what she had done.

As the officer cuffed the man to take him in, he asked the burglar, "Why did you just stand there? All the old lady did was yell a scripture to you."

"Scripture?" replied the burglar. "She said she had an axe and two 38s!"

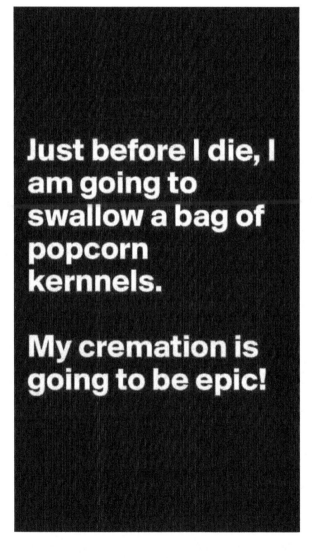

Priceless

Billy Graham was returning to Charlotte after a speaking engagement and when his Plane arrived there was a limousine there to transport him to his home. As he prepared to get into the limo, he stopped and spoke to the driver.

"You know" he said, "I am 87 years old and I have never driven a limousine. Would you mind if I drove it for a while?" The driver said; "No problem, have at it!"

Billy gets into the driver's seat and they head off down the highway. A short distance away sat a rookie State Trooper operating his first speed trap. The long black limo went by him doing 70 in a 55 mph zone.

The trooper pulled out and easily caught the limo, he got out of his patrol car to begin the procedure. The young trooper walked up to the driver's door and when the glass was rolled down, he was surprised to see who was driving.

He immediately excused himself and went back to his car and called his supervisor. He told his supervisor, "I know we are supposed to enforce the law, but I also know that important people are given certain courtesies. I need to know what I should do because I have stopped a very important person."

The supervisor asked, "Is it the governor?"

The young trooper said, "No, he's more important than that."

The supervisor said, "Oh, so it's the President."

The young trooper said, "No, he's even more important than that."

His supervisor finally asked; "Well then, who is it?"

The young trooper said; "'I think it's Jesus, because he's got Billy Graham for a chauffeur!"

Sad News From Minnesota

The Pillsbury Doughboy died yesterday in Minneapolis of a yeast infection and traumatic complications from repeated pokes in the belly. He was 71.

Doughboy was buried in a lightly greased coffin. Dozens of celebrities turned out to pay their respects, including Mrs. Butterworth, Hungry Jack, the California Raisins, Betty Crocker, the Hostess Twinkies, and Captain Crunch. The gravesite was piled high with flours.

Aunt Jemima delivered the eulogy and lovingly described Doughboy as a man who never knew how much he was kneaded.

Born and bred in Minnesota, Doughboy rose quickly in show business, but his later life was filled with turnovers. He was not regarded as a very smart cookie, wasting much of his dough on half-baked schemes. Despite being a little flaky at times, he still was a crusty old man and served as a positive role model for millions.

Doughboy is survived by his wife, Play Dough, three children: John Dough, Jane Dough and Dosey Dough, plus they had one in the oven. He is also survived by his elderly father, Pop Tart.

The funeral was held at 3:50 for about 20 min.

Bumper-Stickers Seen On Military Bases

• 101st Airborne Division-   When it comes to combat, care enough to send the very best. When in doubt, empty the magazine.

• Sniper: You can run, but you'll just die tired!

• Machine Gunners – Accuracy By Volume

• Except For Ending Slavery, Fascism, Nazism and Communism, WAR has never solved anything."

- U.S. Marines – Certified Counselors to the 72 Virgins Dating Club.

- U.S. Air Force – Travel Agents To Allah

- The Marine Corps – When It Absolutely, Positively Has To Be Destroyed Overnight

- Death Smiles At Everyone – Marines Smile Back

- What Do I Feel When I Kill A Terrorist? A Little Recoil

- Marines – Providing Enemies of America an Opportunity To Die For their Country Since 1775

- Life, Liberty and the Pursuit of Anyone Who Threatens It

- Happiness Is A Belt-Fed Weapon

- It's God's Job to Forgive Bin Laden – It was Our Job To Arrange The Meeting

- Artillery Brings Dignity to What Would Otherwise Be Just A Vulgar Brawl

- "One Shot, Twelve Kills – U.S. Naval Gun Fire Support

• My Kid Fought In Iraq So Your Kid Can Party In College and Protest

• A Dead Enemy Is A Peaceful Enemy – Blessed Be The Peacemakers

• If You Can Read This, Thank A Teacher. If You Can Read It In English, Thank A Veteran

• Some people spend an entire lifetime wondering if they made a difference in the world. The U.S. Military doesn't have that problem.

Marijuana issue sent to a joint committee

The Toronto Star 06/14/96

Hospitals resort to hiring doctors

PHYSICIAN SHORTAGE PROMPTING MOVE, ADMINISTRATORS SAY

Art Collector's Wife

A New York attorney representing a wealthy art collector called his client. "I have some good news, and I have some bad news."

The art collector replied, "I've had an awful day. Give me the good news first."

The lawyer said, "Well, I met with your wife today, and she informed me that she just invested $5,000 in two pictures that she thinks will bring a minimum of $15 million to $20 million, and I think she could be right."

Saul replied enthusiastically, "Well done! My wife is a brilliant businesswoman! You've just made my day. Now I know I can handle the bad news. What is it?"

The lawyer replied, "The pictures are of you and your secretary."

Las Vegas Churches Accept Gambling Chips

THIS MAY COME AS A SURPRISE TO THOSE OF YOU NOT LIVING IN LAS VEGAS, BUT THERE ARE MORE CATHOLIC CHURCHES THAN CASINOS

NOT SURPRISINGLY, SOME WORSHIPERS AT SUNDAY SERVICES WILL GIVE CASINO CHIPS RATHER THAN CASH WHEN THE BASKET IS PASSED.

SINCE THEY GET CHIPS FROM MANY DIFFERENT CASINOS, THE CHURCHES HAVE DEVISED A METHOD TO COLLECT THE OFFERINGS.

THE CHURCHES SEND ALL THEIR COLLECTED CHIPS TO A NEARBY FRANCISCAN MONASTERY FOR SORTING AND THEN THE CHIPS ARE TAKEN TO THE CASINOS OF ORIGIN AND CASHED IN.

THIS IS DONE BY THE CHIP MONKS. YOU DIDN'T EVEN SEE IT COMING DID YOU?

HELL EXPLAINED
BY A CHEMISTRY STUDENT

The following is an actual question given on a University of Arizona chemistry mid-term, and an actual answer turned in by a student.

The answer by one student was so 'profound' that the professor shared it with colleagues, via the Internet, which is, of course, why we now have the pleasure of enjoying it as well :

Bonus Question: Is Hell exothermic (gives off heat) or endothermic (absorbs heat)?

Most of the students wrote proofs of their beliefs using Boyle's Law (gas cools when it expands and heats when it is compressed) or some variant.

One student, however, wrote the following:
First, we need to know how the mass of Hell is changing in time. So we need to know the rate at which souls are moving into Hell and the rate at which they are leaving, which is unlikely.. I think that we can safely assume that once a soul gets to Hell, it will not leave. Therefore, no souls are leaving. As for how many souls are entering Hell, let's look at the different religions that exist in the world today.

Most of these religions state that if you are not a member of their religion, you will go to Hell. Since there is more than one of these religions and since people do not belong to more than one religion, we can project that all souls go to Hell. With birth and death rates as they are, we can expect the number of souls in Hell to increase exponentially. Now, we look at the rate of change of the volume in Hell because Boyle's Law states that in order for the temperature and pressure in Hell to stay the same, the volume of Hell has to expand proportionately as souls are added.

This gives two possibilities:

1. If Hell is expanding at a slower rate than the rate at which souls enter Hell, then the temperature and pressure in Hell will increase until all Hell breaks loose.
2. If Hell is expanding at a rate faster than the increase of souls in Hell, then the temperature and pressure will drop until Hell freezes over.
So which is it?

If we accept the postulate given to me by Teresa during my Freshman year that, 'It will be a cold day in Hell before I sleep with you,' and take into account the fact that I slept with her last night, then number two must be true, and thus I am sure that Hell is exothermic and has already frozen over. The corollary of this theory is that since Hell has frozen over, it follows that it is not accepting any more souls and is therefore, extinct. . .leaving only Heaven, thereby proving the existence of a divine being which explains why, last night, Teresa kept shouting "Oh my God."'

THIS STUDENT RECEIVED AN A+.`

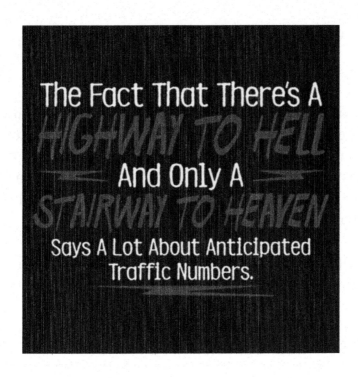

The Fact That There's A
HIGHWAY TO HELL
And Only A
STAIRWAY TO HEAVEN
Says A Lot About Anticipated
Traffic Numbers.

Bugs flying around with wings are flying bugs

By Wayne Hansen
Redwood Co. Extension Educator

"I've got these bugs that look like ants with wings flying around my house. What are they and how do I get rid of them?"

bugs.

Anthracnose continues to develop on many green ash, oak and maple trees. Small spots and blotches are the typical symptoms and are often accompanied by defoliation. NOTE: Do not co

Stupid Title – Dah!

Seven Reasons Not To Mess With Children

A little girl was talking to her teacher about whales. The teacher said it was physically impossible for a whale to swallow a human because even though it was a very large mammal its throat was very small. The little girl stated that Jonah was swallowed by a whale.

Irritated, the teacher reiterated that a whale could not swallow a human; it was physically impossible. The little girl said, "When I get to heaven I will ask Jonah." The teacher asked, "What if Jonah went to hell?" The little girl replied, "Then you ask him."

A Kindergarten teacher was observing her classroom of children while they were drawing. She would occasionally walk around to see each child's work. As she got to one little girl who was working diligently, she asked what the drawing was. The girl replied, "I'm drawing God." The teacher paused and said, "But no one knows what God looks like." Without missing a beat, or looking up from her drawing, the girl replied, "They will in a minute."

A Sunday school teacher was discussing the Ten Commandments with her five and six year olds. After explaining the commandment to honor thy Father and thy Mother, she asked, "Is there a commandment that teaches us how to treat our brothers and sisters?"

From the back, one little boy (the oldest of a family) answered, "Thou shall not kill."

One day a little girl was sitting and watching her mother do the dishes at the kitchen sink. She suddenly noticed that her mother had several strands of white hair sticking out in contrast on her brunette head. She looked at her mother and inquisitively asked, "Why are some of your hairs white, Mum?"
Her mother replied, "Well, every time that you do something wrong and make me cry or unhappy, one of my hairs turns white." The little girl thought about this revelation for a while and then said, "Mummy, how come ALL of grandma's hairs are white?"

The children had all been photographed, and the teacher was trying to persuade them each to buy a copy of the group picture. "Just think how nice it will be to look at it when you are all grown up and say, 'There's Jennifer, she's a lawyer,' or 'That's Michael, He's a doctor.'" A small voice at the back of the room rang out, "And there's the teacher, she's dead."

A teacher was giving a lesson on the circulation of the blood. Trying to make the matter clearer, she said, "Now, class, if I stood on my head, the blood, as you know, would run into it, and I would turn red in the face." "Yes,'" the class said. "Then why is it that while I am standing upright in the ordinary position the blood doesn't run into my feet?" A little fellow shouted, "Cause your feet ain't empty."

What did our parents do to kill boredom before the internet?

I asked my 26 brothers and sisters and they didn't know either.

Adopt A Terrorist Program - Brilliant

The Canadians know how to handle complaints. Here is an example. A Canadian female liberal wrote a lot of letters to the Canadian government, complaining about the treatment of captive insurgents (terrorists) being held in Afghanistan National Correctional System facilities. She demanded a response to her letter. She received back the following reply:

National Defense Headquarters M Gen George R. Pearkes Bldg., 15 NT 101 Colonel By Drive Ottawa ON K1A 0K2 Canada

Dear Concerned Citizen,

Thank you for your recent letter expressing your profound concern of treatment of the Taliban and Al Qaeda terrorists captured by Canadian Forces, who were subsequently transferred to the Afghanistan Government and are currently being held by Afghan officials in Afghanistan National Correctional System facilities.

Our administration takes these matters seriously and your opinions were heard loud and clear here in Ottawa. You will be pleased to learn, thanks to the concerns of citizens like yourself, we are creating a new department here at the Department of National Defense, to be called 'Liberals Accept Responsibility for Killers' program, or L.A.R.K. for short.

In accordance with the guidelines of this new program, we have decided, on a trial basis, to divert several terrorists and place them in homes of concerned citizens such as yourself, around the country, under those citizens personal care. Your personal detainee has been selected and is scheduled for transportation under heavily armed guard to your residence in Toronto next Monday.

Ali Mohammed Ahmed bin Mahmud is your detainee, and is to be cared for pursuant to the standards you personally demanded in your letter of complaint. You will be pleased to know that we will conduct weekly inspections to ensure that your standards of care for Ahmed are commensurate with your recommendations.

Although Ahmed is a sociopath and extremely violent, we hope that your sensitivity to what you described as his 'attitudinal problem' will help him overcome those character flaws. Perhaps you are correct in describing these problems as mere cultural differences. We understand that you plan to offer counselling and home schooling, however, we strongly recommend that you hire some assistant caretakers.

Please advise any Jewish friends, neighbors or relatives about your house guest, as he might get agitated or even violent, but we are sure you can reason with him. He is also expert at making a wide variety of explosive devices from common household products, so you may wish to keep those items locked up, unless in your opinion, this might offend him. Your adopted terrorist is extremely proficient in hand-to-hand combat and can extinguish human life with such simple items as a pencil or nail clippers. We advise that you do not ask him to demonstrate these skills either in your home or wherever you choose to take him while helping him adjust to life in our country.

Ahmed will not wish to interact with you or your daughters except sexually, since he views females as a form of property, thereby having no rights, including refusal of his sexual demands. This is a particularly sensitive subject for him.

You also should know that he has shown violent tendencies around women who fail to comply with the dress code that he will recommend as more appropriate attire. I'm sure you will come to enjoy the anonymity offered by the burka over time. Just remember that it is all part of respecting his culture and religious beliefs' as described in your letter.

You take good care of Ahmed and remember that we will try to have a counsellor available to help you over any difficulties you encounter while Ahmed is adjusting to Canadian culture.

Thanks again for your concern. We truly appreciate it when folks like you keep us informed of the proper way to do our job and care for our fellow man. Good luck and God bless you.

Cordially,
Gordon O'Connor
Minister of National Defense

Trivia

This is a test for us 'older kids'! The answers are printed below, (after the questions) but don't cheat! Answer them first.
1. After the Lone Ranger saved the day and rode off into the sunset, the grateful citizens would ask,

"Who was that masked man?" Invariably, someone would answer, "I don't know, but he left this behind." What did he leave behind?_____
2. When the Beatles first came to the U.S. in early 1964, we all watched them on The __ ___ Show.
3. Get your kicks, __ _____ _____.
4. "The story you are about to see is true. The names have been changed to _____ _ _____."
5. "In the jungle, the mighty jungle, ____ ____ ____ ____."
6. After the Twist, The Mashed Potato, and the Watusi, we 'danced' under a stick that was lowered as low as we could go in a dance called the '_____.'
07. "Nestle's makes the very best.... _____."
08. Satchmo was America 's 'Ambassador of Goodwill.' Our parents shared this great jazz trumpet player with us. His name was ;

_____ _____.
9. What takes a licking and keeps on ticking?

_____.
10. Red Skelton's hobo character was named _____ ___ _____ and Red always ended his television show by saying, "Good Night, and _____ _____."
11. Some Americans who protested the Vietnam War did so by burning their _____ _____.
12. The cute little car with the engine in the back and the trunk in the front was called the VW. What other names did it go by? ___ & _____.

13. In 1971, singer Don MacLean sang a song about, 'the day the music died.' This was a tribute to _____ _____.

14. We can remember the first satellite placed into orbit. The Russians did it. It was called _____.

15. One of the big fads of the late 50's and 60's was a large plastic ring that we twirled around our waist. It was called the _____ _____.

16. Remember LS/MFT _____ _____/_____ _____ _____?

17. Hey Kids! What time is it? It's _____ _____ _____!

18. Who knows what secrets lie in the hearts of men? Only the _____ knows!

19. There was a song that came out in the 60's that was "a grave yard smash". Its name was the _____ _____!

20. Alka Seltzer used a "boy with a tablet on his head" as its Logo/Representative. What was the boy's name? _____

ANSWERS

1. The Lone Ranger left behind a silver bullet.
2. The Ed Sullivan Show
3. On Route 66
4. To protect the innocent.
5. The Lion Sleeps Tonight
6. The limbo
7. Chocolate
8. Louis Armstrong

9. The Timex watch
10. Freddy, The Freeloader and "Good Night and God Bless."
11. Draft cards (Bras were also burned. Not flags, as some have guessed)
12. Beetle or Bug
13. Buddy Holly
14. Sputnik
15. Hoola-hoop
16. Lucky Strike/Means Fine Tobacco
17. Howdy Doody Time
18. Shadow
19. Monster Mash;
20. Speedy

Football Fans

An elementary teacher starts a new job at a school in San Francisco and, trying to make a good impression on her first day, explains to her class that she's a Raiders fan. She asks the class to raise their hands if they too are Raiders fans.

Everyone in the class raises their hand except one little girl. The teacher looks at the girl with surprise and says, "Mary, why didn't you raise your hand?"

Because I'm not a Raiders fan," she replied.

The teacher, still shocked, asked: "Well, if you're not a Raiders fan, then who do you support?"

"I'm a Chargers fan, and proud of it," Mary replied.

The teacher could not believe her ears. "Mary, why are you a Chargers fan?" "Because my mom and dad are from San Diego, and my mom is a Chargers fan and my dad is a Chargers fan, so I'm a Chargers fan too!"

"Well," said the teacher, in a obviously annoyed tone, "that's no reason for you to be a Chargers fan. You don't have to be just like your parents all of the time. What if your mom was a prostitute and your dad was a drug addict and a car thief, what would you be then?"

Mary said, "Then I'd be a Raiders fan."

Retirement

You can retire to Phoenix, Arizona where
1. You are willing to park three blocks away from your house because you found shade.
2. You've experienced condensation on your rear-end from the hot water in the toilet bowl.
3. You can drive for four hours in one direction and never leave town.
4. You have over 100 recipes for Mexican food.
5. You know that "dry heat" is comparable to what hits you in the face when you open your oven door at 500 degrees.
6. The four seasons are: tolerable, hot, really hot, and ARE YOU KIDDING ME?

OR

You can retire to California where
1. You make over $450,000 and you still can't afford to buy a house.
2. The fastest part of your commute is going down your driveway.
3. You know how to eat an artichoke.
4. When someone asks you how far something is, you tell them how long it will take to get there rather than how many miles away it is.
5. The four seasons are: Fire, Flood, Mud and Drought.

OR

You can retire to New York City where
1 You say "the city" and expect everyone to know you mean Manhattan.
2. You can get into a four-hour argument about how to get from Columbus Circle to Battery Park, but can't find Wisconsin on a map.
3. You think Central Park is "nature."
4. You believe that being able to swear at people in their own language makes you multilingual.
5. You've worn out a car horn. (IF you have a car.)
6. You think eye contact is an act of aggression

OR

You can retire to Minnesota where
1. You only have three spices: salt, pepper and ketchup.
2. Halloween costumes have to fit over parkas.
3. You have seventeen recipes for casserole.
4. Sexy lingerie is anything flannel with less than eight buttons.
5. The four seasons are: almost winter, winter, still winter, and road repair.
6. The highest level of criticism is "He is different," "She is different," or "It was different!"

OR

You can retire to The Deep South where
1. You can rent a movie and buy bait in the same store.
2 "Y'all" is singular and "all y'all" is plural.
3. "He needed killin'" is a valid defense.
4. Everyone has two first names: Billy Bob, Jimmy Bob, Joe Bob, Betty Jean, Mary Beth, etc.
5. Everything is either: "in yonder," "over yonder" or "out yonder."
6. You can say anything about anyone, as long as you say "Bless his heart" at the end!

OR

You can move to Colorado where
1. You carry your $3,000 mountain bike atop your $500 car.

2. You tell your husband to pick up Granola on his way home, so he stops at the day care center.
3. A pass does not involve a football or dating.
4. The top of your head is bald, but you still have a pony tail.

OR

You can retire to Nebraska or Kansas where
1. You've never met any celebrities, but the mayor knows your name.
2. Your idea of a traffic jam is three cars waiting to pass a tractor.
3. You have had to switch from "heat" to "A/C" on the same day.
4. You end sentences with a preposition--"Where's my coat at?"

OR

FINALLY you can retire to Florida where.
1. You eat dinner at 3:15 in the afternoon.
2. All purchases include a coupon of some kind - even houses and cars.
3. Everyone can recommend an excellent cardiologist, dermatologist, proctologist, podiatrist, or orthopedist.
4. Road construction never ends anywhere in the state.
5. Cars in front of you often appear to be driven by headless people.

Meeting on open meetings is closed

Homicide victims rarely talk to police

Starvation can lead to health hazards

DEAR DR. DONOHUE: My weight is totally over the top. I am 5 feet 7 inches tall and weigh close to 3 0 0 pounds. I was average weight in high

difficult to meet daily protein, vitamin and mineral requirements.

Get to a dietitian for diet advice that provides for essential nutrients while paring down calorie intake sensibly. Your local hospital should be able to put you on the track of one. Combine

MY WIFE SAID I NEVER LISTEN TO HER, OR SOMETHING LIKE THAT

WallingfordSign.com f

The Cowboy

A cowboy, who just moved to Wyoming from Texas walks into a bar and orders three mugs of Bud. He sits in the back of the room, drinking a sip out of each one in turn. When he finishes them, he comes back to the bar and orders three more.

The bartender approaches and tells the cowboy, "You know, a mug goes flat after I draw it. It would taste better if you bought one at a time."

The cowboy replies, "Well, you see, I have two brothers. One is in Arizona, the other is in Colorado. When we all left our home in Texas, we promised that we'd drink this way to remember the days when we drank together. So I'm drinking one beer for each of my brothers and one for myself." The bartender admits that this is a nice custom, and leaves it there.

The cowboy becomes a regular in the bar, and always drinks the same way. He orders three mugs and drinks them in turn.

One day, he comes in and only orders two mugs. All the regulars take notice and fall silent. When he comes back to the bar for the second round, the bartender says, "I don't want to intrude on your grief, but I wanted to offer my condolences on your loss."

The cowboy looks quite puzzled for a moment, then a light dawns in his eyes and he laughs. "Oh, no, everybody's just fine," he explains, "It's just that my wife and I joined the Baptist Church and I had to quit drinking. Hasn't affected my brothers though."

Male or Female?

You might not have known this, but a lot of non-living objects are actually either male or female. Here are some examples:

FREEZER BAGS: They are male, because they hold everything in, but you can see right through them.

PHOTOCOPIERS: These are female, because once

turned off; it takes a while to warm them up again. They are an effective reproductive device if the right buttons are pushed, but can also wreak havoc if you push the wrong buttons.

TIRES: Tires are male, because they go bald easily and are often over inflated.

HOT AIR BALLOONS: Also a male object, because to get them to go anywhere, you have to light a fire under their butt.

SPONGES: These are female, because they are soft, squeezable and retain water.

WEB PAGES: Female, because they're constantly being looked at and frequently getting hit on.

TRAINS: Definitely male, because they always use the same old lines for picking up people.

EGG TIM ERS: Egg timers are female because, over time, all the weight shifts to the bottom.

HAMMERS: Male, because in the last 5000 years, they've hardly changed at all, and are occasionally handy to have around.

THE REMOTE CONTROL: Female. Ha! You probably thought it would be male, but consider this: It easily gives a man pleasure, he'd be lost without it, and while he doesn't always know which buttons to push, he just keeps trying.

Mayberry

The reason Mayberry was so peaceful and quiet was because nobody was married. Andy, Aunt Bea, Barney, Floyd, Howard, Goober, Gomer, Sam, Earnest T Bass, Helen, Thelma Lou, Clara and, of course, Opie were all single. The only married person was Otis, and he stayed drunk.

The Atheist In the Woods

An atheist was walking through the woods. "What majestic trees! What powerful rivers! What beautiful animals," he said to himself.

Suddenly, he heard a rustling in the bushes behind him. He turned to look and saw a 7-foot grizzly bear charging towards him. He ran as fast as he could along the path. He looked over his shoulder and saw that the bear was closing on him. He looked over his shoulder again, and the bear was even closer! And then, he tripped and fell.

Rolling over to pick himself up, he found the bear was right on top of him, reaching towards him with its left paw, and raising the right paw to strike.

At that instant the Atheist cried out, "Oh my God!" Time stopped. The bear froze. The forest was silent. A bright light shone upon the man, and a voice came out of the sky.

"You deny My existence for all these years. You teach others I don't exist and even credit creation to a cosmic accident. Do you expect me to help you out of this predicament? Am I to count you as a believer?"

The atheist looked directly into the light. "It would be hypocritical of me to suddenly ask you to treat me as a Christian now, but perhaps you could make the BEAR a Christian?"

There was a pause.

"Very well," said the voice. The light went out. The sounds of the forest resumed. The bear dropped his right arm, brought both paws together, bowed his head and spoke, "Lord, bless this food, which I am about to receive. Amen."

Just One Letter

A young monk arrives at the monastery. He is assigned to helping the other monks in copying the old canons and laws of the church, by hand. He notices, however, that all of the monks are copying from copies, not from the original manuscript. So, the new monk goes to the Old Abbot to question this, pointing out that if someone made even a small error in the first copy, it would never be picked up! In fact, that error would be continued in all of the subsequent copies.

The head monk, says, "We have been copying from the copies for centuries, but you make a good point, my son."

He goes down into the dark caves underneath the monastery where the original manuscripts are held as archives, in a locked vault that hasn't been opened for hundreds of years. Hours go by and nobody sees the Old Abbot.

So, the young monk gets worried and goes down to look for him. He sees him banging his head against the wall and wailing.

"We missed the R! We missed the R! We missed the bloody R!" His forehead is all bloody and bruised and he is crying uncontrollably.

The young monk asks the old Abbot, "What's wrong, Father?"

With a choking voice, the old Abbot replies, "The word was. . .CELEBRATE!"

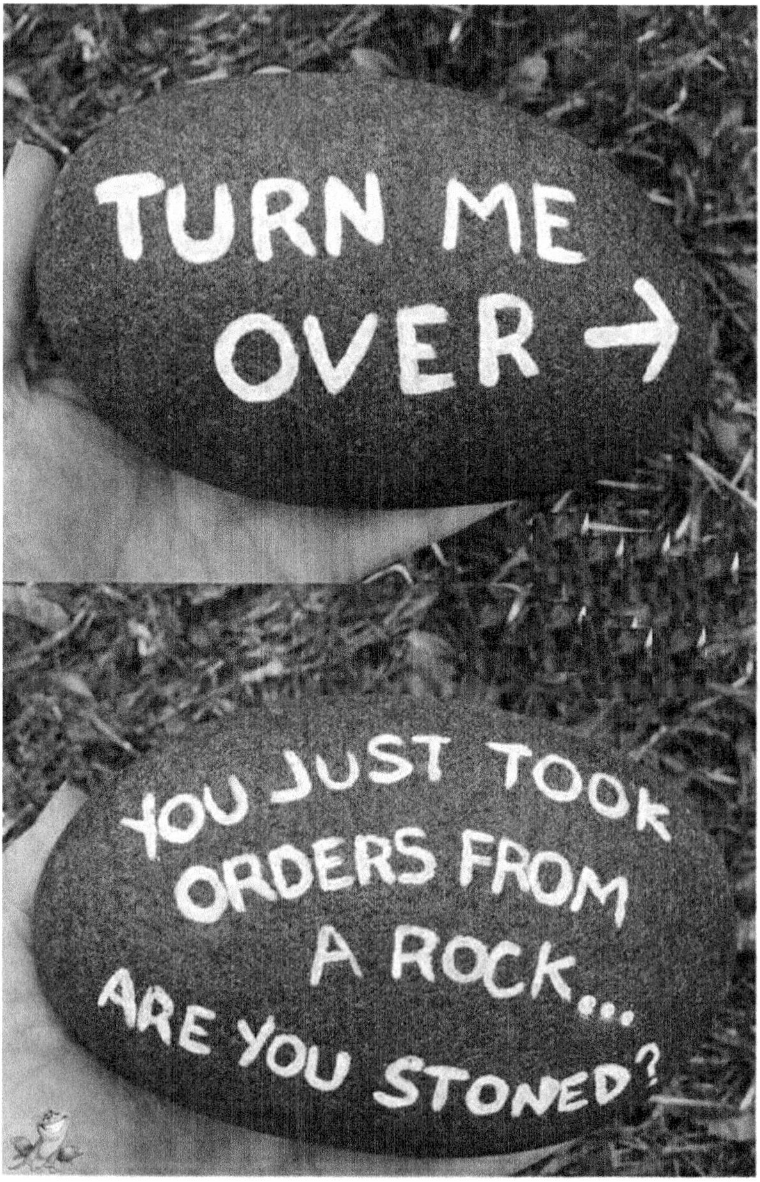
TURN ME OVER →
YOU JUST TOOK ORDERS FROM A ROCK...
ARE YOU STONED?

Women Aboard Ships

The Department of the Navy is now assigning females to quarters in a separate private "OFF LIMITS" area on all aircraft carriers. Addressing all boat personnel at Pearl, CINCPAC advised, "Female sleeping quarters will be "out-of-bounds" for all males. Anyone caught breaking this rule will be fined $50 the first time." He continued, "Anyone caught breaking this rule the second time will be fined $150. Being caught a third time will cost you a fine of $500. Are there any questions?"

At this point, a Marine from the security detail assigned to the ship stood up in the crowd and inquired, "How much for a season pass?"

Court Testimony

If you ever get to testify in court, you might wish you could have been as sharp as this policeman. He was being cross-examined by a defense attorney during a felony trial. The lawyer was trying to undermine the police officer's credibility.

Q: "Officer, did you see my client fleeing the scene?"
A: "No, sir. But I subsequently observed a person matching the description of the offender, running several blocks away."

Q: "Officer, who provided this description?"
A: "The officer who responded to the scene."

Q: "A fellow officer provided the description of this so-called offender. Do you trust your fellow officers?"
A: "Yes, sir. With my life."
Q: "With your life? Let me ask you this then officer. Do you have a room where you change your clothes in preparation for your daily duties?"
A: "Yes sir, we do!"

Q: "And do you have a locker in the room?"
A: "Yes, sir, I do."

Q: "And do you have a lock on your locker?"
A: "Yes, sir."

Q: "Now, why is it, officer, if you trust your fellow officers with your life, you find it necessary to lock your locker in a room you share with these same officers?"
A: "You see, sir, we share the building with the court complex, and sometimes lawyers have been known to walk through that room."

The courtroom exploded with laughter, and a prompt recess was called!

File missing

Windows cannot find the file.
Would you like some wine instead?

Yes   No

THE OLDER CROWD

A distraught senior citizen phoned her doctor's office. "Is it true," she wanted to know, "that the medication you prescribed has to be taken for the rest of my life?"

"Yes, I'm afraid so," the doctor told her. There was a moment of silence before the senior lady replied, "I'm wondering, then, just how serious is my condition, because this prescription is marked, 'No Refills.'"

SURGERY

An older gentleman was on the operating table awaiting surgery and he insisted that his son, a renowned surgeon, perform the operation. As he was about to get the anesthesia, he asked to speak to his son. "Yes, Dad, what is it?" "Don't be nervous, son; do your best, and just remember, if it doesn't go well, if something happens to me, your mother is going to come and live with you and your wife."

Old Age is NOT for Sissies

This is what all of you 70+ year olds, and yet-to-be kids have to look forward to!! This is something that happened at an assisted living center.

The people who lived there have small apartments but they all eat at a central cafeteria. One morning one of the residents didn't show up for breakfast so my wife went upstairs and knocked on his door to see if everything was Okay. She could hear him through the door and he said that he was running late and would be down shortly so she went back to the dining area.

An hour later he still hadn't arrived so she went back up towards his room and she found him on the stairs. He was coming down the stairs but was having a rough time. He had a death grip on the hand rail and seemed to have trouble getting his legs to work right. She told him she was going to call an ambulance but he told her no, he wasn't in any pain and just wanted to have his breakfast. So she helped him the rest of the way down the stairs and he had his breakfast.

When he tried to return to his room he was completely unable to get up even the first step so they called an ambulance for him. A couple hours later she called the hospital to see how he was doing. The receptionist there said he was fine, he just had both of his legs in one leg of his boxer shorts.

Younger Generation Wedding

Dearest Dad,

I am coming home to get married soon, so get your check book out. I'm in love with a boy who is far away from me. As you know, I am presently living in Australia, and he lives in Scotland. We met on a dating website, became friends on Facebook, had long chats on Whatsapp. He proposed to me on Skype, and now we've had two months of a relationship through Viber. My beloved and favorite Dad, I need your blessing, good wishes, and a really big wedding.

Lots of love and thanks.

Your favorite daughter,

Lilly

DAD'S RESPONSE:

My Dearest Lilly,

Like Wow! Really? Cool!

I suggest you two get married on Twitter, have a
honeymoon on Tango, buy your kids on Amazon,
and pay for it all through PayPal. And when you
get fed up with this new husband, sell him on eBay.

Love,
Your Dad

The Redhead

A man is dining in a fancy restaurant and there's a
gorgeous redhead sitting at the next table. He's been
checking her out since he sat down, but lacks the
nerve to talk with her.

Suddenly she sneezes, and her glass eye comes
flying out of its socket toward the man. He
reflexively reaches out, grabs it out of the air, and
hands it back.

"Oh my, I am so sorry," the woman says as she pops
her eye back in place. "Let me buy your dinner to
make it up to you," she says.

They enjoy a wonderful dinner together, and
afterwards they go to the theatre followed by drinks.

They talk, they laugh, she shares her deepest dreams and he shares his. She listens. After paying for everything, she asks him if he would like to come to her place for a nightcap.

They had a wonderful time. He stays for breakfast. The next morning, she cooks a gourmet meal with all the trimmings.

The guy is amazed. Everything had been SO incredible!

"You know," he said, "you are the perfect woman. Are you this nice to every guy you meet?"

"No," she replies, "You just happened to catch my eye."

Dear John

A Marine stationed in Afghanistan recently received a "Dear John" letter from his girlfriend back home. It read as follows:

Dear Ricky,
I can no longer continue our relationship. The distance between us is just too great. I must admit that I have cheated on you twice, since you've been gone, and it's not fair to either of us. I'm sorry.

Please return the picture of me that I sent to you.
Love, Becky

The Marine, with hurt feelings, asked his fellow Marines for any snapshots they could spare of their girlfriends, sisters, ex-girlfriends, aunts, cousins etc. In addition to the picture of Becky, Ricky included all the other pictures of the pretty gals he had collected from his buddies. There were 57 photos in that envelope, along with this note:

Dear Becky,
I'm so sorry, but I can't quite remember who you are. Please take your picture from the pile, and send the rest back to me.

Take Care, Ricky

Murder at Costco

Tired of constantly being broke and stuck in an unhappy marriage, a young husband decided to solve both problems by taking out a large insurance policy on his wife with himself as the beneficiary and then arranging to have her killed.

A 'friend of a friend' put him in touch with a nefarious dark-side underworld figure who went by the name of 'Artie.' Artie explained to the husband that his going price for snuffing out a spouse was $10,000.

The husband said he was willing to pay that amount but that he wouldn't have any cash on hand until he could collect his wife's insurance money. Artie insisted on being paid at least something up front, so the man opened his wallet, displaying the single dollar coin that rested inside. Artie sighed, rolled his eyes and reluctantly agreed to accept the dollar as down payment for the dirty deed.

A few days later, Artie followed the man's wife to the local Costco Supermarket. There, he surprised her in the produce department and proceeded to strangle her with his gloved hands. As the poor unsuspecting woman drew her last breath and slumped to the floor, the manager of the produce department stumbled unexpectedly onto the murder scene. Unwilling to leave any living witnesses behind, ol' Artie had no choice but to strangle the produce manager as well.

However, unknown to Artie, the entire proceedings were captured by the hidden security cameras and observed by the shop's security guard, who immediately called the police. Artie was caught and arrested before he could even leave the premises.

Under intense questioning at the police station, Artie revealed the whole sordid plan, including his unusual financial arrangements with the hapless husband who was also quickly arrested.

The next day in the newspaper, the headline declared

"ARTIE CHOKES 2 for $1.00 @ Costco"

I GOT MY CONCEALED CARRY PERMIT YESTERDAY MORNING

In the afternoon, I went over to the local Bass Pro Shop to get a 9mm handgun for home/personal protection. When I was ready to pay for the pistol and ammo, the cashier said, "Strip down, facing me."

Making a mental note to complain to the NRA about the gun control wackos running wild, I did just as she had instructed.

When the hysterical shrieking and alarms finally subsided, I found out she was referring to how I should place my credit card in the card reader!

As a senior citizen, I do not get flustered often, but this time it took me a while to get my pants back on. I have been asked to shop elsewhere in the future. They need to make their instructions to seniors a little more clear. I still don't think I looked that bad! Just need to wear underwear more often.

EXERCISE FOR PEOPLE OVER 60

Begin by standing on a comfortable surface, where you have plenty of room at each side.

With a 5-lb potato bag in each hand, extend your arms straight out from your sides and hold them there as long as you can. Try to reach a full minute, and then relax.

Each day you'll find that you can hold this position for just a bit longer.

After a couple of weeks, move up to 10-lb potato bags. Then try 50-lb potato bags and eventually try to get to where you can lift a 100-lb potato bag in each hand and hold your arms straight for more than a full minute. (I'm at this level).

After you feel confident at that level, put a potato in each bag.

BREAKING NEWS: The Chicago Police Dept has replaced all sirens with the National Anthem, to force suspects to stop running and take a knee.

Will I Live To See 80?

Here's something to think about. I recently picked a new primary care doctor. After two visits and exhaustive Lab tests, he said I was doing 'fairly well' for my age. (I just turned "seventy-ish"). A little concerned about that comment, I couldn't resist asking him, "Do you think I'll live to be 80?"

He asked, "Do you smoke tobacco, or drink beer, wine or hard liquor?"
"Oh no," I replied. "I'm not doing drugs, either!"

Then he asked, "Do you eat rib-eye steaks and barbecued ribs?"

I said, "Not much... my former doctor said that all red meat is very unhealthy!"

"Do you spend a lot of time in the sun, like playing golf, boating, sailing, hiking, or bicycling?"

"No, I don't," I said.

He asked, "Do you gamble, drive fast cars, or have lots of sex?"

"No," I said.

He looked at me and said, "Then, why do you even care?"

Philosophers of the Past Century

~ Betsy Salkind: Men are like linoleum floors. Lay'em right and you can walk all over them for thirty years.

Jean Kerr: The only reason they say 'Women and children first' is to test the strength of the lifeboats.

Prince Philip: When a man opens a car door for his wife, it's either a new car or a new wife.

Emo Philips: A computer once beat me at chess, but it was no match for me at kickboxing.

Harrison Ford: Wood burns faster when you have to cut and chop it yourself.

Spike Milligan: The best cure for Sea Sickness, is to sit under a tree.

Jean Rostand: Kill one man and you're a murderer, kill a million and you're a conqueror.

Arnold Schwarzenegger: Having more money doesn't make you happier. I have 50 million dollars but I'm just as happy as when I had 48 million.

WH Auden: We are here on earth to do good unto others. What the others are here for, I have no idea.

Jonathan Katz: In hotel rooms, I worry. I can't be the only guy who sits on the furniture naked.

Johnny Carson: If life were fair, Elvis would still be alive today and all the impersonators would be dead.

Warren Tantum: I don't believe in astrology. I am a Sagittarius and we're very skeptical.

Steve Martin: Hollywood must be the only place on earth where you can be fired by a man wearing a Hawaiian shirt and a baseball cap.

Jimmy Durante: Home cooking--where many a man thinks his wife is.

Doug Hanwell: America is so advanced that even the chairs are electric.

George Roberts: The first piece of luggage on the carousel never belongs to anyone.

Jonathan Winters: If God had intended us to fly He would have made it easier to get to the airport.

Robert Benchley: I have kleptomania, but when it gets bad, I take something for it.

John Glenn: As I hurtled through space, one thought kept crossing my mind - every part of this rocket was supplied by the lowest bidder.

David Letterman: America is the only country where a significant proportion of the population believes that professional wrestling is real but the moon landing was faked.

Howard Hughes: I'm not a paranoid, deranged millionaire. I'm a billionaire.

LARRY MAY BECOME MY NEW FAVORITE STUDENT!

A new teacher was trying to make use of her psychology courses. She started her class by saying, "Everyone who thinks they're stupid, stand up!" After a few seconds, Little Larry stood up. The teacher said, "Do you think you're stupid, Larry?" "No, ma'am, but I hate to see you standing there all by yourself!"

Larry watched, fascinated, as his mother smoothed cold cream on her face. "Why do you do that, Mommy?" he asked. "To make myself beautiful," said his mother, who then began removing the cream with a tissue. "What's the matter, asked Larry, "Giving up?"

The math teacher saw that Larry wasn't paying attention in class. She called on him and said, "Larry! What are 2 and 4 and 28 and 44?" Larry quickly replied, "NBC, FOX, ESPN and the Cartoon Network!"

Larry's kindergarten class was on a field trip to their local police station where they saw pictures tacked to a bulletin board of the 10 most wanted criminals. One of the youngsters pointed to a picture and asked if it really was the photo of a wanted person. "Yes," said the policeman. "The detectives want very badly to capture him." Larry asked, "Why didn't you keep him when you took his picture?"

Little Larry attended a horse auction with his father. He watched as his father moved from horse to horse, running his hands up and down the horse's legs and rump, and chest. After a few minutes, Larry asked, "Dad, why are you doing that?" His father replied, "Because when I'm buying horses, I have to make sure that they are healthy and in good shape before I buy." Larry, looking worried, said, "Dad, I think the UPS guy wants to buy Mom."

STORIES

A Lesson in Irony

The Food Stamp Program, administered by the U.S. Department of Agriculture, is proud to be distributing this year the greatest amount of free meals and food stamps ever, to 46 million people.

Meanwhile, the National Park Service, administered by the U.S. Department of the Interior, asks us "Please Do Not Feed the Animals." Their stated reason for the policy is because "the animals will grow dependent on handouts and will not learn to take care of themselves."

An Incredible Way to Look at God

When God solves our problems, we have faith in His abilities. When God doesn't solve our problems, He has faith in our abilities. God's accuracy may be observed in the hatching of eggs.

-those of the canary in 14 days
-those of the barnyard hen in 21 days
-eggs of ducks and geese in 28 days
-those of the mallard in 35 days
-those of the parrot and the ostrich in 42 days

(Notice, they are all
divisible by seven, the number of days in a week!)

God's wisdom is seen in the making of an elephant. The four legs of this great beast all bend forward in the same direction. No other quadruped is so made. God planned that this animal would have a huge body--too large to live on two legs. For this reason He gave it four fulcrums so that it can rise from the ground easily.

The horse rises from the ground on its two front legs first. A cow rises from the ground with its two hind legs first.

How wise the Lord is in all His works of creation! Each watermelon has an even number of stripes on the rind. -Each orange has an even number of segments. Each ear of corn has an even number of rows. Each stalk of wheat has an even number of grains. Every bunch of bananas has on its lowest row an even number of bananas, and each row decreases by one, so that one row has an even number and the next row an odd number.

Amazing

The waves of the sea roll in on shore twenty-six to the minute in all kinds of weather. All grains are found in even numbers on the stalks. God has caused the flowers to blossom at certain specified times during the day. Linnaeus, the great botanist, once said that if he had a conservatory containing the right kind of soil, moisture and temperature, he could tell the time of day or night by the flowers that were open and those that were closed.

The lives of each of us may be ordered by the Lord in a beautiful way for His glory, if we will only entrust Him with our life. If we try to regulate our own life, it will only be a mess and a failure. Only God, who made our brain and heart, can successfully guide them to a profitable end.

Interesting

A while back, when I told General Krulak, the former Commandant of the Marine Corps, now the chair of the Naval Academy Board of Visitors, that we were having General Mattis speak, he said, "Let me tell you a Jim Mattis story." General Krulak said, when he was Commandant of the Marine Corps, every year, starting about a week before Christmas, he and his wife would bake hundreds and hundreds and hundreds of Christmas cookies. They would package them in small bundles.

Then on Christmas day, he would load his vehicle. At about 4 a.m., General Krulak would drive himself to every Marine guard post in the Washington-Annapolis-Baltimore area and deliver a small package of Christmas cookies to whatever Marines were pulling guard duty that day. He said that one year, he had gone down to Quantico as one of his stops to deliver Christmas cookies to the

Marines on guard duty. He went to the command center and gave a package to the lance corporal who was on duty.

He asked, "Who's the officer of the day?" The Lance Corporal said, "Sir, it's Brigadier General Mattis." And General Krulak said, "No, no, no. I know who General Mattis is. I mean, who's the officer of the day today, Christmas day?" The Lance Corporal, feeling a little anxious, said, "Sir, it is Brigadier General Mattis."

General Krulak said that, about that time, he spotted in the back room a cot, or a daybed. He said, "No, Lance Corporal. Who slept in that bed last night?" The lance corporal said, "Sir, it was Brigadier General Mattis."

About that time, General Krulak said that General Mattis came in, in a duty uniform with a sword, and General Krulak said, "Jim, what are you doing here on Christmas day? Why do you have duty?" General Mattis told him that the young officer who was scheduled to have duty on Christmas day had a family, and General Mattis decided it was better for the young officer to spend Christmas Day with his family, and so he chose to have duty on Christmas Day.

General Krulak said, "That's the kind of officer that Jim Mattis is."

The story above was told by Dr. Albert C. Pierce, the Director of the Center for the Study of Professional Military Ethics at The United States Naval Academy. He was introducing General James Mattis who gave a lecture on Ethical Challenges in Contemporary Conflict in the spring of 2006. This was taken from the transcript of that lecture.

Don't Widen the Plate

In Nashville, Tennessee, during the first week of January, 1996, more than 4,000 baseball coaches descended upon the Opryland Hotel for the 52nd annual ABCA's convention. While I waited in line to register with the hotel staff, I heard other more veteran coaches rumbling about the lineup of speakers scheduled to present during the weekend. One name, in particular, kept resurfacing, always with the same sentiment — "John Scolinos is here? Oh, man, worth every penny of my airfare.

Who is John Scolinos, I wondered. No matter, I was just happy to be there.

In 1996, Coach Scolinos was 78 years old and five years retired from a college coaching career that began in 1948. He shuffled to the stage to an impressive standing ovation, wearing dark polyester pants, a light blue shirt, and a string around his neck from which home plate hung — a full-sized, stark-white home plate. Seriously, I wondered, who is this guy?

After speaking for twenty-five minutes, not once mentioning the prop hanging around his neck, Coach Scolinos appeared to notice the snickering among some of the coaches. Even those who knew Coach Scolinos had to wonder exactly where he was going with this, or if he had simply forgotten about home plate since he'd gotten on stage.

Then finally, "You're probably all wondering why I'm wearing home plate around my neck," he said, his voice growing irascible. I laughed along with the others, acknowledging the possibility. "I may be old, but I'm not crazy. The reason I stand before you today is to share with you baseball people what I've learned in my life, what I've learned about home plate in my 78 years." Several hands went up when Scolinos asked how many Little League coaches were in the room.

"Do you know how wide home plate is in Little League? After a pause, someone offered, "Seventeen inches?," more of a question than answer. "That's right," he said. "How about in Babe Ruth's day? Any Babe Ruth coaches in the house?" Another long pause. "Seventeen inches?" a guess from another reluctant coach. "That's right," said Scolinos. "Now, how many high school coaches do we have in the room?" Hundreds of hands shot up, as the pattern began to appear. "How wide is home plate in high school baseball? "Seventeen inches," they said, sounding more confident. "You're right!" Scolinos barked. "And you college coaches, how wide is home plate in college?" "Seventeen inches!" we said, in unison. "Any Minor League coaches here? How wide is home plate in pro ball?" "Seventeen inches! "RIGHT! And in the Major Leagues, how wide home plate is in the Major Leagues?" "Seventeen inches!" "SEV-EN-TEEN INCHES!" he confirmed, his voice bellowing off the walls. "And what do they do with a Big League pitcher who can't throw the ball over seventeen inches?" Pause. "They send him to Pocatello !" he hollered, drawing raucous laughter. "What they don't do is this: they don't say, 'Ah, that's okay, Jimmy. You can't hit a seventeen-inch target? We'll make it eighteen inches or nineteen inches. We'll make it twenty inches so you have a better chance of hitting it. If you can't hit that, let us know so we can make it wider still, say twenty-five inches.'"

Pause. "Coaches…" pause, "… what do we do when our best player shows up late to practice? When our team rules forbid facial hair and a guy shows up unshaven? What if he gets caught drinking? Do we hold him accountable? Or do we change the rules to fit him? Do we widen home plate? The chuckles gradually faded as four thousand coaches grew quiet, the fog lifting as the old coach's message began to unfold. He turned the plate toward himself and, using a Sharpie, began to draw something. When he turned it toward the crowd, point up, a house was revealed, complete with a freshly drawn door and two windows. "This is the problem in our homes today. With our marriages, with the way we parent our kids. With our discipline. We don't teach accountability to our kids, and there is no consequence for failing to meet standards. We widen the plate!"

Pause. Then, to the point at the top of the house he added a small American flag. "This is the problem in our schools today. The quality of our education is going downhill fast and teachers have been stripped of the tools they need to be successful, and to educate and discipline our young people. We are allowing others to widen home plate! Where is that getting us?"

Silence. He replaced the flag with a Cross. "And this is the problem in the Church, where powerful people in positions of authority have taken advantage of young children, only to have such an atrocity swept under the rug for years. Our church leaders are widening home plate for themselves! And we allow it."

"And the same is true with our government. Our so called representatives make rules for us that don't apply to themselves. They take bribes from lobbyists and foreign countries. They no longer serve us. And we allow them to widen home plate and we see our country falling into a dark abyss while we watch."

I was amazed. At a baseball convention where I expected to learn something about curve balls and bunting and how to run better practices, I had learned something far more valuable. From an old man with home plate strung around his neck, I had learned something about life, about myself, about my own weaknesses and about my responsibilities as a leader. I had to hold myself and others accountable to that which I knew to be right, lest our families, our faith, and our society continue down an undesirable path.

"If I am lucky," Coach Scolinos concluded, "you will remember one thing from this old coach today. It is this: if we fail to hold ourselves to a higher standard, a standard of what we know to be right; if we fail to hold our spouses and our children to the same standards, if we are unwilling or unable to provide a consequence when they do not meet the standard; and if our schools and churches and our government fail to hold themselves accountable to those they serve, there is but one thing to look forward to."

With that, he held home plate in front of his chest, turned it around, and revealed its dark black backside, "… dark days ahead."

Coach Scolinos died in 2009 at the age of 91, but not before touching the lives of hundreds of players and coaches, including mine. Meeting him at my first ABCA convention kept me returning year after year, looking for similar wisdom and inspiration from other coaches. He is the best clinic speaker the ABCA has ever known because he was so much more than a baseball coach. His message was clear: "Coaches, keep your players—no matter how good they are—your own children, your churches, your government, and most of all, keep yourself at seventeen inches."

And this my friends is what our country has become and what is wrong with it today, and how to fix it. "Don't widen the plate."

The Wonderful Powers
And Uses For WD~40

What a product, and I thought it was mostly for squeaky doors! WD-40: who knew!

I had a neighbor who bought a new pickup. I got up very early one Sunday morning and saw that omeone had spray painted red all around the sides of this beige truck (for some unknown reason). I went over, woke him up, and told him the bad news. He was very upset and was trying to figure out what to do—probably nothing until Monday morning, since nothing was open. Another neighbor came out and told him to get his WD-40 and clean it off. It removed the unwanted paint beautifully and did not harm his paint job that was on the truck. I was impressed!

WD-40 who knew? "Water Displacement #40". The product began from a search for a rust preventative solvent and degreaser to protect missile parts. WD-40 was created in 1953, by three technicians at the San Diego Rocket Chemical Company. Its name comes from the project that was to find a 'Water Displacement' Compound. They were finally successful for a formulation, with their fortieth attempt, thus WD-40. The 'Convair Company' bought it in bulk to protect their atlas missile parts. Ken East (one of the original founders) says there is nothing in WD-40 that would hurt you.

When you read the 'shower door' part, try it. It's the first thing that has ever cleaned that spotty shower door. If yours is plastic, it works just as well as on glass. It's a miracle! Then try it on your stove-top. It's now shinier than it's ever been. You'll be amazed.

WD-40 Uses:
1. Protects silver from tarnishing.
2. Removes road tar and grime from cars.
3. Cleans and lubricates guitar strings.
4. Gives floor that 'just-waxed' sheen without making them slippery.
5. Keeps the flies off of Cows, Horses, and other Farm Critters, as well. (Ya' gotta' love this one!!!)
6. Restores and cleans chalkboards.
7. Removes lipstick stains.
8. Loosens stubborn zippers.
9. Untangles jewelry chains.
10. Removes stains from stainless steel sinks.
11. Removes dirt and grime from the barbecue grill.
12. Keeps ceramic / terracotta garden pots from oxidizing.
13. Removes tomato stains from clothing.
14. Keeps glass shower doors free of water spots.
15. Camouflages scratches in ceramic and marble floors.
16. Keeps scissors working smoothly.
17. Lubricates noisy door hinges on both home and vehicles doors.
18. It removes that nasty tar and scuff marks from the kitchen flooring. It doesn't seem to harm the finish and you won't have to scrub nearly as hard to get them off. Just remember to open some windows if you have a lot of marks.
19. Remove those nasty bug guts that will eat away the finish on your car if not removed quickly!
20. Gives a children's playground gym slide a shine

for a super fast slide.

21. Lubricates gearshift and mower deck lever for ease of handling on riding mowers.

22. Rids kids rocking chair and swings of squeaky noises.

23. Lubricates tracks in sticking home windows and makes them easier to open.

24. Spraying an umbrella stem makes it easier to open and close.

25. Restores and cleans padded leather dashboards in vehicles, as well as vinyl bumpers.

26. Restores and cleans roof racks on vehicles.

27. Lubricates and stops squeaks in electric fans.

28. Lubricates wheel sprockets on tricycles, wagons, and bicycles for easy handling.

29. Lubricates fan belts on washers and dryers and keeps them running smoothly.

30. Keeps rust from forming on saws and saw blades, and other tools.

31. Removes grease splatters from stove-tops.

32. Keeps bathroom mirror from fogging.

33. Lubricates prosthetic limbs.

34. Keeps pigeons off the balcony (they hate the smell).

35. Removes all traces of duct tape.

36. Folks even spray it on their arms, hands, and knees to relieve arthritis pain.

37. Florida's favorite use is: 'cleans and removes love bugs from grills and bumpers.'

38. The favorite use in the state of New York, it protects the Statue of Liberty from the elements.

39. WD-40 attracts fish. Spray a little on live bait or lures and you will be catching the big one in no time. Also, it's a lot cheaper than the chemical attractants that are made for just that purpose. Keep in mind though, using some chemical laced baits or lures for fishing are not allowed in some states.
40. Use it for fire ant bites. It takes the sting away immediately and stops the itch.
41. It is great for removing crayon from walls. Spray it on the marks and wipe with a clean rag.
42. Also, if you've discovered that your teenage daughter has washed and dried a tube of lipstick with a load of laundry, saturate the lipstick spots with WD-40 and rewash. Presto! The lipstick is gone!
43. If you spray it inside a wet distributor cap, it will displace the moisture, allowing the engine to start.

P. S.
As for that basic, main ingredient? It's FISH OIL.

Mayo Clinic on Drinking Water

A cardiologist determined that heart attacks can be triggered by dehydration. Good thing to know from The Mayo Clinic. How many folks do you know who say they don't want to drink anything before going to bed because they'll have to get up during the night?

Heart attack and water: Drinking one glass of water before going to bed avoids stroke or heart attack.

I asked my doctor why people need to urinate so much at night time. Answer from my cardiac doctor: Gravity holds water in the lower part of your body when you are upright (legs swell). When you lie down and the lower body (legs and etc.) seeks level with the kidneys, it is then that the kidneys remove the water because it is easier. I knew you need your minimum water to help flush the toxins out of your body, but this was news to me.

Correct time to drink water--very important and from a cardiac specialist! Drinking water at a certain time maximizes its effectiveness in the body. Two glasses of water after waking up helps activate internal organs.
One glass of water 30 minutes before a meal helps digestion.
One glass of water before taking a bath helps lower blood pressure.
One glass of water before going to bed avoids stroke or heart attack
One glass of water at bed time will also help prevent night time leg cramps. Your leg muscles are seeking hydration when they cramp and wake you up with a Charlie Horse.
Mayo Clinic on aspirin -Dr. Virend Somers is a cardiologist from the Mayo Clinic who is the lead

author of the report in the July 29, 2008 issue of the Journal of the American College of Cardiology. Most heart attacks occur in the day, generally between 6 A.M. and noon. Having one during the night, when the heart should be most at rest, means that something unusual happened. Somers and his colleagues have been working for a decade to show that sleep apnea is to blame.

1. If you take an aspirin or a baby aspirin once a day, take it at night. The reason: aspirin has a 24-hour "half-life"; therefore, if most heart attacks happen in the wee hours of the morning, the Aspirin would be strongest in your system.

2. Aspirin lasts a really long time in your medicine chest; for years. (when it gets old, it smells like vinegar).

Something that we can do to help ourselves. Bayer is making crystal aspirin to dissolve instantly on the tongue. They work much faster than the tablets.

Why keep aspirin by your bedside? It's about heart attacks. There are other symptoms of a heart attack, besides the pain on the left arm. One must also be aware of an intense pain on the chin, as well as nausea and lots of sweating; however, these symptoms may also occur less frequently.

Note: There may be NO pain in the chest during a heart attack.

The majority of people (about 60%) who had a heart attack during their sleep did not wake up. However, if it occurs, the chest pain may wake you up from your deep sleep. If that happens, immediately dissolve two aspirins in your mouth and swallow them with a bit of water. Then call 911. Phone a neighbor or a family member who lives very close by. Say "heart attack!" Say that you have taken 2 aspirins. Take a seat on a chair or sofa near the front door, and wait for their arrival and DO NOT LIE DOWN!

FROM ONE FRIEND TO ANOTHER

This is by Andy Rooney, a man who had the gift of saying so much with so few words.

I've learned. . .
-That the best classroom in the world is at the feet of an elderly person.
-That when you're in love, it shows.
-That just one person saying to me, 'You've made my day!' makes my day.
-That having a child fall asleep in your arms is one of the most peaceful feelings in the world.
-That being kind is more important than being right.
-That I can always pray for someone when I don't have the strength to help him in any other way.
- That no matter how serious your life requires you to be, everyone needs a friend to act goofy with.
-That sometimes all a person needs is a hand to hold and a heart to understand
- That simple walks with my father around the block

on summer nights when I was a child did wonders for me as an adult.

-That life is like a roll of toilet paper. The closer it gets to the end, the faster it goes.

-That money doesn't buy class.

-That it's those small daily happenings that make life so spectacular.

-That under everyone's hard shell is someone who wants to be appreciated and loved.

-That to ignore the facts does not change the facts.

-That when you plan to get even with someone, you are only letting that person continue to hurt you.

-That love, not time, heals all wounds.

-That the easiest way for me to grow as a person is to surround myself with people smarter than I am.

-That everyone you meet deserves to be greeted with a smile.

-That no one is perfect until you fall in love with them.

-That life is tough, but I'm tougher.

-That opportunities are never lost; someone will take the ones you miss.

-That when you harbor bitterness, happiness will dock elsewhere.

-That I wish I could have told my Mom that I love her one more time before she passed away.

-That one should keep his words both soft and tender, because tomorrow he may have to eat them.

-That a smile is an inexpensive way to improve your looks.

-That when your newly born grandchild holds your little finger in his little fist, you're hooked for life.

-That everyone wants to live on top of the mountain, but all the happiness and growth occurs while you're climbing it.

-That the less time I have to work with, the more things I get done.

Bananas and Milk Duds

Below is an article written by Rick Reilly of *Sports Illustrated*. He details his experiences when given the opportunity to fly in a F-14 Tomcat. If you aren't laughing out loud by the time you get to 'Milk Duds', your sense of humor is seriously broken.

This message is for America's most famous athletes. Someday you may be invited to fly in the back seat of one of your country's most powerful fighter jets. Many of you already have. John Elway, John Stockton, Tiger Woods to name a few. If you get this opportunity, let me urge you, with the greatest sincerity--Move to Guam!

Change your name. Fake your own death! Whatever you do, Do Not Go!!! I know.

The U.S. Navy invited me to try it. I was thrilled. I was pumped. I was toast! I should've known when they told me my pilot would Be Chip (Biff) King of Fighter Squadron 213 at Naval Air Station Oceana in Virginia Beach.

Whatever you're thinking a Top Gun named Chip (Biff) King looks like, triple it. He's about six-foot, tan, ice-blue eyes, wavy surfer hair, finger-crippling handshake -- the kind of man who wrestles dyspeptic alligators in his leisure time. If you see this man, run the other way. Fast.

Biff King was born to fly. His father, Jack King, was for years the voice of NASA missions. ('T-minus 15 seconds and counting'. Remember?) Chip would charge neighborhood kids a quarter each to hear his dad. Jack would wake up from naps surrounded by nine-year-olds waiting for him to say, 'We have lift off'.

Biff was to fly me in an F-14D Tomcat, a ridiculously powerful $60 million weapon with nearly as much thrust as weight, not unlike Colin Montgomerie. I was worried about getting airsick, so the night before the flight I asked Biff if there was something I should eat the next morning.

"Bananas," he said. "For the potassium?" I asked. "'No," Biff said, "because they taste about the same coming up as they do going down."

The next morning, out on the tarmac, I had on my flight suit with my name sewn over the left breast. (No call sign -- like Crash or Sticky or Lead foot. But, still, very cool.) I carried my helmet in the crook of my arm, as Biff had instructed.

A fighter pilot named Psycho gave me a safety briefing and then fastened me into my ejection seat, which, when employed, would 'egress' me out of the plane at such a velocity that I would be immediately knocked unconscious.

Just as I was thinking about aborting the flight, the canopy closed over me, and Biff gave the ground crew a thumbs-up In minutes we were firing nose up at 600 mph. We leveled out and then canopy-rolled over another F-14.

Those 20 minutes were the rush of my life. Unfortunately, the ride lasted 80. It was like being on the roller coaster at Six Flags Over Hell. Only without rails. We did barrel rolls, snap rolls, loops, yanks and banks. We dived, rose and dived again, sometimes with a vertical velocity of 10,000 feet per minute. We chased another F-14, and it chased us.

We broke the speed of sound. Sea was sky and sky was sea. Flying at 200 feet we did 90-degree turns at 550 mph, creating a G force of 6.5, which is to say I felt as if 6.5 times my body weight was smashing against me, thereby approximating life as Mrs. Colin Montgomerie.

And I egressed the bananas. And I egressed the pizza from the night before. And the lunch before that. I egressed a box of Milk Duds from the sixth grade. I made Linda Blair look polite. Because of the G's, I was egressing stuff that never thought would be egressed. I went through not one airsick bag, but two.

Biff said I passed out. Twice. I was coated in sweat. At one point, as we were coming in upside down in a banked curve on a mock bombing target and the G's were flattening me like a tortilla and I was in and out of consciousness, I realized I was the first person In history to throw down.

I used to know 'cool'. Cool was Elway throwing a touchdown pass, or Norman making a five-iron bite. But now I really know 'cool'. Cool is guys like Biff, men with cast-iron stomachs and freon nerves. I wouldn't go up there again for Derek Jeter's black book, but I'm glad Biff does every day, and for less a year than a rookie reliever makes in a home stand.

A week later, when the spins finally stopped, Biff called. He said he and the fighters had the perfect call sign for me. Said he'd send it on a patch for my flight suit.

What is it? I asked. "Two Bags."

"A veteran is someone who at one point in their life, wrote a blank check made payable to The United States of America for any amount, up to and including their life."

Interesting Confusions

1. Can u cry under water?
2. Do fishes ever get thirsty?
3. Why dont birds fall off tress when they sleep
4. Why is it called building when it is already built?
5. When they say dogs food is new and improved, who tastes it?
6. If money doesnt grow on trees, why do banks have branches?
7. Why does round pizza come in a square box?
8. Why doesnt glue stick to its bottle?

CRAZY WORLD ISNT IT?

What God Did at Pearl Harbor

What God did at Pearl Harbor that day is interesting. Tour boats ferry people out to the USS Arizona Memorial in Hawaii every thirty minutes.

We just missed a ferry and had to wait thirty minutes. I went into a small gift shop to kill time. In the gift shop, I purchased a small book entitled, "Reflections on Pearl Harbor" by Admiral Chester Nimitz.

Sunday, December 7th, 1941, Admiral Chester Nimitz was attending a concert in Washington, DC. He was paged and told there was a phone call for him. When he answered the phone, it was President Franklin Delano Roosevelt on the phone. He told Admiral Nimitz that he (Nimitz) would now be the Commander of the Pacific Fleet.

Admiral Nimitz flew to Hawaii to assume command of the Pacific Fleet. He landed at Pearl Harbor on Christmas Eve, 1941. There was such a spirit of despair, dejection and defeat. You would have thought the Japanese had already won the war.

On Christmas Day, 1941, Adm. Nimitz was given a boat tour of the destruction wrought on Pearl Harbor by the Japanese. Big sunken battleships and Navy vessels cluttered the waters everywhere you looked.

As the tour boat returned to dock, the young helmsman of the boat asked, "Well Admiral, what do you think after seeing all this destruction?"

Admiral Nimitz's reply shocked everyone within the sound of his voice. Admiral Nimitz said, "The Japanese made three of the biggest mistakes an attack force could ever make, or God was taking care of America. Which do you think it was?"

Shocked and surprised, the young helmsman asked, "What do mean by saying the Japanese made the three biggest mistakes an attack force ever made?"

Nimitz explained: Mistake number one: The Japanese attacked on Sunday morning. Nine out of every ten crewmen of those ships were ashore on leave. If those same ships had been lured to sea and been sunk--we would have lost 38,000 men instead of 3,800.

Mistake number two: When the Japanese saw all those battleships lined in a row, they got so carried away sinking those battleships, they never once bombed our dry docks opposite those ships.
If they had destroyed our dry docks, we would have had to tow every one of those ships to America to be repaired. As it is now, the ships are in shallow water and can be raised. One tug can pull them over to the

dry docks, and we can have them repaired and at sea by the time we could have towed them to America. And I already have crews ashore anxious to man those ships.

Mistake number three: Every drop of fuel in the Pacific theater of war is in top of the ground storage tanks five miles away over that hill. One attack plane could have strafed those tanks and destroyed our fuel supply.

That's why I say the Japanese made three of the biggest mistakes an attack force could make or God was taking care of America.

I've never forgotten what I read in that little book. It is still an inspiration as I reflect upon it. In jest, I might suggest that because Admiral Nimitz was a Texan, born and raised in Fredericksburg, Texas, he was a born optimist. But any way you look at it, Admiral Nimitz was able to see a silver lining in a situation and circumstance where everyone else saw only despair and defeat.

President Roosevelt had chosen the right man for the right job. We desperately needed a leader that could see silver linings in the midst of the clouds of dejection, despair and defeat.

WE DID NOT SEE THIS IN THE AMERICAN NEWS MEDIA

The most memorable moment from the trip in Israel of President Trump and the First Lady was probably that moment at the entrance to the house of President Rivlin.

The following article was written by - George Deek from *The Jewish Standard*

"Nechama Rivlin, President Rivlin's wife, welcomed the First Lady Melania Trump at the door. As they were about to walk inside, Nechama whispered to Melania that she will do her best to catch up with the walking pace, but she might be a bit slower because of her medical condition which requires her to use an oxygen tank. Melania took her hand, looked at her and said: "We'll walk at any pace you choose."

And so they walked, slowly, gracefully and proudly, hand in hand.

That, is the moment I choose to cherish. That silent gesture has neither any political significance nor any colorful tone to it, but it is everything.

It is the hope we yearn for when we speak of peace. It is the kindness we wish to protect when we speak of defeating terror. It is the dignity we want to teach when we speak of stopping hate. It is the friendship we pray for when we speak of our unbreakable bond. In other words, this gesture encompasses everything that is good, kind and human.

Twelve Short Stories

1. I interviewed my grandmother for part of a research paper I'm working on for my Psychology class. When I asked her to define success in her own words, she said, "Success is when you look back at your life and the memories make you smile."

2. I asked my mentor - a very successful business man in his 70's what his top three tips are for success. He smiled and said, "Read something no one else is reading, think something no one else is thinking, and do something no one else is doing."

3. After my 72 hour shift at the fire station, a woman ran up to me at the grocery store and gave me a hug. When I tensed up, she realized I didn't recognize her. She let go with tears of joy in her eyes and the most sincere smile and said, "On 9-11-2001, you carried me out of the World Trade Center."

4. After I watched my dog get run over by a car, I sat on the side of the road holding him and

crying. And just before he died, he licked the tears off my face.

5. At 7AM, I woke up feeling ill, but decided I needed the money, so I went into work. At 3PM I got laid off. On my drive home I got a flat tire. When I went into the trunk for the spare, it was flat too. A man in a BMW pulled over, gave me a ride, we chatted, and then he offered me a job. I start tomorrow.

6. As my father, three brothers, and two sisters stood around my mother's hospital bed, my mother uttered her last coherent words before she died. She simply said, "I feel so loved right now. We should have gotten together like this more often."

7. I kissed my dad on the forehead as he passed away in a small hospital bed. About five seconds after he passed, I realized it was the first time I had given him a kiss since I was a little boy.

8. In the cutest voice, my 8-year-old daughter asked me to start recycling. I chuckled and asked, "Why?" She replied, "So you can help me save the planet." I chuckled again and asked, "And why do you want to save the planet?" "Because that's where I keep all my stuff," she said.

9. When I witnessed a 27-year-old breast cancer patient laughing hysterically at her 2-year-old daughter's antics, I suddenly realized that, I need to stop complaining about my life and start celebrating it again.

10. A boy in a wheelchair saw me desperately struggling on crutches with my broken leg and offered to carry my backpack and books for me. He helped me all the way across campus to my class and as he was leaving he said, "I hope you feel better soon."

11. I was feeling down because the results of a biopsy came back malignant. When I got home, I opened an e-mail that said, "Thinking of you today. If you need me, I'm a phone call away." It was from a high school friend I hadn't seen in ten years.

12. I was traveling in Kenya and I met a refugee from Zimbabwe. He said he hadn't eaten anything in over three days and looked extremely skinny and unhealthy. Then my friend offered him the rest of the sandwich he was eating. The first thing the man said was, "We can share it."

The best sermons are lived, not preached

The Corvette

A man named Tom Nicholson posted on his Facebook account the sports car that he had just bought and how a man approached and told him that the money used to buy this car could've fed thousands of less fortunate people.

His response to this man made him famous on the Internet. Read his story as stated on Facebook.

A guy looked at my Corvette the other day and said, "I wonder how many people could have been fed for the money that sports car cost."

I replied I am not sure; it fed a lot of families in Bowling Green, Kentucky who built it. It fed the people who make the tires, the people who made the components that went into it, the people in the copper mine who mined the copper for the wires, the people in Decatur IL at Caterpillar who make the trucks that haul the copper ore.

It fed the trucking people who hauled it from the plant to the dealer and fed the people working at the dealership and their families.

BUT, I have to admit, I guess I really don't know how many people it fed.

That is the difference between capitalism and welfare mentality.

When you buy something, you put money in people's pockets and give them dignity for their skills.

When you give someone something for nothing, you rob them of their dignity and self-worth.

Capitalism is freely giving your money in exchange for something of value.

Socialism is taking your money against your will and shoving something down your throat that you never asked for.

Words and Simple Wisdom from Roy

I want to say something about the spirituality debate. You don't believe in God? Okay, but why is it so important for many of you to mock those of us that do?

If we're wrong, what have we lost when we die? Nothing! How does our faith in Jesus Christ bring you any harm? You think it makes me stupid? Gullible? Ignorant? That's okay too. How does that affect you? If you're wrong your consequence is far worse.

I would rather live my life believing in God and serving Him, and find out I was right, than not believe in Him and not serve Him, and find out I was wrong. Then it's too late.

Ain't no shame in my game! I believe in Jesus Christ. He said deny me in front of your friends and I will deny you in front of my Father.

A Poem to Which We Can Relate

I remember the corned beef of my Childhood,
And the bread that we cut with a knife,
When the Children helped with the housework,
And the men went to work not the wife.

The cheese never needed a fridge,
And the bread was so crusty and hot,
The Children were seldom unhappy,
And the Wife was content with her lot.

I remember the milk from the bottle,
With the yummy cream on the top,
Our dinner came hot from the oven,
And not from a freezer; or shop.

The kids were a lot more contented,
They didn't need money for kicks,
Just a game with their friends in the road,
And sometimes the Saturday flicks.

I remember the shop on the corner,
Where biscuits for pennies were sold
Do you think I'm a bit too nostalgic?
Or is it....I'm just getting Old?
Bathing was done in a wash tub,
With plenty of rich foamy suds
But the ironing seemed never ending
As Mum pressed everyone's 'duds'.

I remember the slap on my backside,
And the taste of soap if I swore
Anorexia and diets weren't heard of
And we hadn't much choice what we wore.

Do you think that bruised our ego?
Or our initiative was destroyed?
We ate what was put on the table
And I think life was better enjoyed.

Author, Unknown

Civilization in 2017

Our Phones – Wireless
Cooking - Fireless
Cars - Keyless
Food - Fatless
Tires -Tubeless
Dress - Sleeveless
Youth - Jobless
Leaders - Shameless

Relationships - Meaningless
Attitudes - Careless
Babies - Fatherless
Feelings - Heartless
Education - Valueless
Children – Mannerless

We are-SPEECHLESS,
Government-is CLUELESS,
And our Politicians-are WORTHLESS!

I'm scared.

Family and
Friends
In
2017

It's been a glorious year for us, and we feel particularly blessed with our family and friends.

Dahk and Jan at The General Morgan Inn on Easter with Peter Cottontail!

Our daughter Dr. Kheri with sons Jace and Kalib.

Daughter-in-law Julie
in a conversation!

Our friend Sherrie Ottinger (rt.)
With her sister Lesa

Friend and
talented
artist Amy
Foshee

Theresa and Ed Henry. Theresa is one of the first people we met when we came to East Tennessee. She does Jan's hair and is awesome!

Grandson Alex Knox (rt.) as one of the coaches at Satellite High School in Florida.

Daughter Kheri with Diane Lowery. Diane is co-owner and glass-blowing artist of Lowery's Hot Glass in Old Town San Diego. Her creations are as beautiful as she is! And check them out at www.loweryshotglass.com. The store is at 3985 Harney St. Phone 619-297-3473

Grandson Alex Knox
with his girlfriend Sage.
Looks like love, huh?

Jan as pensive. Wonder what's
going on in that head!

Boyfriend Sean Ross
with daughter Kheri
out having fun on a
sunny California day!

Long-time Greeneville friend Diane Nellessen on the beach in California. Diane was one of the first people we met when we moved to Tennessee.

Granddaughter Lexi Knox showing her Certificate after completing her training in Phlebotomy. She was offered a job before she even finished the training!

Dahk. . . well, being Dahk!

Eva Samms looking like she's just having WAY too much fun!

Good pals of ours, Craig and Sherrie Ottinger.

Our daughter Kheri with long-time, dear friend (and still a cutey!) Lisa Hoffman

Craig Ottinger (top), and Bob and Jackie Jenkins. We just met Bob and Jackie this year—they're great people and loads of fun to be around!

Now our friend Dave Fountaine LOOKS serious here, but trust us, we don't think he has a serious bone in his body!

Jim Sams. When he's got a smile this big, you KNOW he's up to something!

Jan and Sweet Pea Brenda Triplett. Looks Like they're solving world issues!

Rose and Crawford Smith celebrated their 68th wedding anniversary this year! Wow!

Dick with wife Susie Van Buren. Dick received a Quilt of Valor this year for his military service.

Kalib, Kheri, and Jace Henry maybe having WAY too much fun!

Daughter Kheri with boyfriend Sean Ross.

Theresa Henry with her dad at Brumley's Christmas Day! It's always a good day when her dad is visiting!

Our friends, Ben and Susan Weems' daughter, Mikayla (center holding the ball) is the goalie on Greeneville's Galaxy Team. And we might add that she is a most excellent goalie!

Julie and Warren Knox
In Montenegro.

Our son Warren looking buff!

Alex Knox and girlfriend Sage at
A University of Central Florida football game.

Julie Knox in Montenegro on the Serbian border.

Our son Warren on a Time Out

Dear and sweet friends from Brumley's Restaurant Brenda Triplett and Wayne Horton (also known as Mr. General Morgan Inn!)

Sisters Mikayla and Abigail Weems enjoying the pool at Myrtle Beach.

Our best Ohio friends Marsha Reichenbaugh and Mary Inbody. They're in front of Wittich's Candy Shop, which is the nation's oldest family owned candy store. They've been in business for 177 years!!!

Mary Inbody and Marsha Reichenbach with friends
at the pumpkin display at the Circleville (Ohio)
Pumpkin Show.

Our dog Haley in our family cemetery by Scooter's grave. They were the best of friends. We always referred to them as the Two Amigos.

Jan and Dahk at Myers Pumpkin Patch.

A dead tree in our meadow with turkey buzzards in it. Could be a Halloween card, huh?

Our sweetheart Haley

Then our sweetheart Molly

And our little sweetheart Rosie

The Breakfast Club

Ya gotta understand: this whole Breakfast Club thing started very innocently several years ago with just three friends meeting for breakfast a couple of times a week.

As time went by, more people were invited. Then, when Jan had to wake up Dahk on those days, she described it to him as, "You need to get up—we have Breakfast Club this morning." (It was way easier getting him up when the thought of food was involved!) Thus, the gathering of friends now had a name!

However, just because there is a name for this group, please don't start thinking that this is some kind of exclusive, muckity-muck club! Within this group, we are known to have solved U.S. and world problems, however, no one else is listening!

So, we have become content in our comings together, celebrating that we made it to another week! We laugh a lot, are known to randomly sing a Good Morning song to friends AND strangers, have breakfast birthday and anniversary parties—all while keeping the staff at the restaurant either working or entertained. Take a look at the following pictures and you'll see what we mean!

Starting at Left and working up: Jim Sams, Joanne Anderson, Barb Evans Amy Foshie, Jan Knox, Jackie Jenkins. Then Bob Jenkins, Lisa Kyker, Craig Ottinger, Dave Fountaine, and Eva Sams. We're at Gina's Family Restaurant on Rt. 107.

Different day, different group! Left side: Susie Van Buren, Bob Jenkins, Lisa Kyker. Right top: Jan, Dahk, Jackie Jenkins, and Dick Van Buren.

Now keep in mind while you peruse through these pictures, we never really know for sure how many folks will show up each time. It could be as few as three, or as many as 20, if it's someone's birthday! Most times, it's between 6 and 10.

Lisa Kyker and Sherrie Ottinger serving birthday carrot cake made by Jessica at Gina's Family Restaurant. By the way, it is the BEST carrot cake in the UNIVERSE! Order one for you by calling Gina's! Phone 423-787-7991

Jan showing the iron decorative hooks Craig Ottinger made for her. He is so talented!

Jim and Eva Sams, and Jan. Don't let the sweet looks fool you— they're probably up to something!

Ronnie Rader, Dahk, Cotton Davis, and Horace Davis. We're not real sure how all this got started, (or maybe we're just not sayin'), but these guys are collectively known as **The Caney Branch Mafia!** Dahk met them at Aunt Bea's Restaurant where the Breakfast Club meets most of the time. Caney Branch Mafia was mentioned, and zap, that's it! So he guys made it official with T-shirts and hats! They don't DO anything, but they all think it's cool to be called that! (It sometimes takes so little to entertain the boys!)

Dahk and Ronnie Rader probably having an impromptu discussion with the CBM members!

Dahk's proud moment getting his CBM shirt!

I Know, I know . . . these boys are something else!

Dave Fountaine and Jan solving world problems at the Breakfast Club.

Horace Davis, Jan, and Craig Ottinger being entertained by someone!

A contemplation moment for Jan and Dahk?
Probably not!

Jim Sams, Eva Sams, and Bob Jenkins.

Starting at bottom left: Dick and Susie Van Bren, Sherrie and Craig Ottinger, Dave Fountaine, Diana Nellison, Jim Sams, Jan and Dahk.

Sherrie Ottinger, known as the Dirt Girl. Want to know garden/yard stuff? Sherrie's your girl!

The very pretty and always delightful Lisa Kyker!

Gina, owner of Gina's Family Restaurant on 107 in Greeneville, and one of the meeting places of the Breakfast Club.

Special visitors Marsha Reichenbaugh and Mary Inbody from Ohio (in the foreground) and Faye and Marty Stephens from Illinois (back center and right).

Dick Van Buren
and Sherrie Ottinger
showing him his
birthday cake for
his 83rd birthday!
We told him he is
now older than dirt
and 2 weeks
younger than water!
We love you Dick!

Something must be funny!

Jan celebrating her birthday with the Breakfast Club. She's already got icing on her lips and face!

Bob Jenkins sharing his wisdom with us. Don't believe it even for a minute!

Ya know that stuff I just said about Bob Jenkins on the last page? Same thing goes for Dahk here!

Bob and Jackie Jenkins seeming to be so serious. Must be deciding what to have for breakfast!

The Caney Branch Mafia in uniform: Dahk Knox,
Horace Davis, Cotton Davis, Ronnie Rader, and
new member and hitman Craig Ottinger

And Some We'll Miss

Paul Meade

See the smile here on Paul's face? That's pretty much the way you always saw him—and he'd be the one to make you laugh. We met him and his wife Wilma at church and shared many-a-potluck party times with them.

Dr. Jasper (Jappy) Hedges

This man, known to Jan as Dr. Hedges, was the doctor who brought Jan into this world! He was our family doctor until he retired! He died this year at 100 years old!

Jan and his daughter, Ann, were classmates throughout our school years, so Jan spent time around him at his house also. He was an easy-to-talk-to doctor, and all-round good guy. There will always be fond memories of him.

Sandy Russell

Oh what a delight Sandy was to anyone who had the blessing of knowing her! She was a volunteer at DeBusk Elementary School. Her specialty? The smile that was always on her face, and sharing a hug with friends.

Scooter Knox

Scooter Booter (as we called him) was a dream dog that came true. He was a drop-off dog, and whoever dumped him out of their car gave us a real life blessing. He took on the role of obsessive-compulsive guard dog, and even went so far as to sleep in our library where he could see out the front and side windows. Nobody got past him, and he taught this skill to our other dogs as well. He learned about being loved, liked it, and got a bunch of it. What a great little guy!

Oh So

Southern

Yep, this is the fun chapter. Stick your nose up in the air like you're someone snooty (that's the way we put it here). Then give your head that "uppity" toss! Okay, you've got it!

Now, get prepared to be put in your place, 'cause this chapter ain't about THOSE uppity snooty people. THIS chapter is about the redder people of the south, known as Rednecks! Yep, wear the badge proudly!

Extreme Redneckness

You're An EXTREME Redneck when

1. You let your 14-year-old daughter smoke at the dinner table in front of her kids.

2. The Blue Book value of your truck goes up and down depending on how much gas is in it.

3. You've been married three times and still have the same in-laws.

4. You think a woman who is out of your league bowls on a different night.

5. You wonder how service stations keep their restrooms so clean.

6. Someone in your family died right after saying, 'Hey, bubba, watch this.'

7. You think Dom Perignon is a Mafia leader.

8. Your wife's hairdo was once ruined by a ceiling fan.

9. Your junior prom offered day care.

10. You think the last words of the Star-Spangled Banner are 'Gentlemen, start your engines.'

11. You lit a match in the bathroom and your house exploded right off its wheels.

12. The Halloween pumpkin on your porch has more teeth than your spouse.

13. You have to go outside to get something from the fridge.

14. One of your kids was born on a pool table.

15. You can't get married to your sweetheart because there's a law against it.

16. You think loading the dishwasher means getting your wife drunk.

Quite the TV tray, huh?

Yes, that's an oven on the back of the car! Hey, yah might be
in Tennessee.

Designer bumper!

Can you believe they're driving it? Don't laugh, it works.

For some things, there are no words! Hey! Yah do what cha can from keepin' from goin' out in the snow.

And speaking of toilets . .

Wait . . . we might know this guy!

Kin?

Two good ol' boys in a Alabama trailer park were sitting around talking one afternoon over a cold beer after getting off work at the local Nissan plant.

After a while, the first guy says to the second, "If'n I was to sneak over to your trailer Saturday and make love to your wife while you was off huntin', and she got pregnant and had a baby, would that make us kin?"

The second guy crooked his head sideways for a minute, scratched his head and squinted his eyes thinking real hard about the question. Finally, he says, "Well, I don't know about kin, but it would make us even!"

Politically
Incorrect

Finally, we got back to a Republican being elected. Praise the Lord that we survived those years of Obama (sorry dem friends)! And now, with a new president, we see absolutely no reason to stop this chapter now! And hey, if President Trump is not politically correct, why should we be?

Just Thought You Should Know

The year was 1947. Some of you will recall that and many of you are too young to have recalled, however the following is TRUE!

On July 8, 1947, numerous witnesses claim that an Unidentified Flying Object, (UFO), with five aliens aboard, crashed onto a sheep and mule ranch just outside Roswell, New Mexico.

This is a well-known incident that many say has long been covered-up by the U.S. Air Force, as well as other Federal agencies and organizations.

However, what you may NOT know is that in the month of April, year 1948, nine months after the alien crash, the following people were born:

Barrack Obama Sr.
Albert A. Gore, Jr.
Hillary Rodham
William J. Clinton
John F. Kerry
Howard Dean
Nancy Pelosi
Dianne Feinstein
Charles E. Schumer
Barbara Boxer
Joe Biden

This is the obvious consequence of aliens breeding with sheep and jack-asses. I truly hope this bit of information clears up a lot of things for you. It did for me. Now you can stop wondering why they support the bill to help all Illegal Aliens.

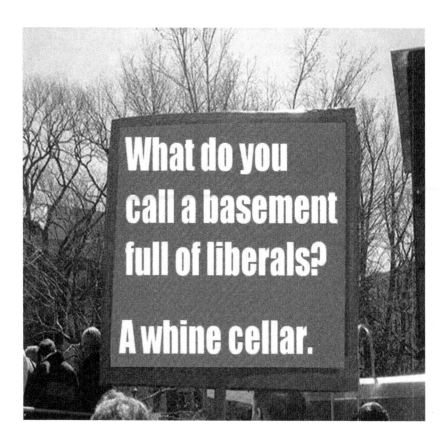

Gotta Love Texas Women!

This was written by a 21 year-old female who gets it. It's her future she's worried about and this is how she feels about the social welfare big government state that she lives in! These solutions are just common sense in her opinion.

This was in the Waco Tribune Herald, Waco, TX.

PUT ME IN CHARGE

Put me in charge of food stamps. No cash for Ding Dongs or Ho Ho's, just money for 50-pound bags of rice and beans, blocks of cheese and all the powdered milk you can haul away. If you want steak and frozen pizza, then get a job.

Put me in charge of Medicaid. Then, we'll test recipients for drugs, alcohol, and nicotine. If you want to use drugs, alcohol, or smoke, then get a job.

Put me in charge of government housing. Ever live in a military barracks? You will maintain our property in a clean and good state of repair. Your "home" will be subject to inspections anytime and possessions will be inventoried. If you want a plasma TV or Xbox 360, then get a job and your own place.

In addition, you will either present a check stub from a job each week or you will report to a "government" job. It may be cleaning the roadways of trash, painting and repairing public housing, whatever we find for you. We will sell your 22-inch rims and low profile tires and your blasting stereo and speakers and put that money toward the "common good."

Before you write that I've violated someone's rights, realize that all of the above is voluntary. If you want our money, accept our rules. Before you say that this would be "demeaning" and ruin their "self-esteem," consider that it wasn't that long ago that taking someone else's money for doing absolutely nothing was demeaning and lowered self-esteem.

If we are expected to pay for other people's mistakes we should at least attempt to make them learn from their bad choices. The current system rewards them for continuing to make bad choices.

And while you are on government subsistence, you no longer can VOTE! Yes, that is correct. For you to vote would be a conflict of interest. You will voluntarily remove yourself from voting while you are receiving a government welfare check. If you want to vote, then get a job.

Isn't it weird that in America our flag and our culture offend so many people, but our benefits don't?

The most amazing part of this well written piece is the fact Maureen Dowd, a very liberal columnist from the New York Times wrote it!

Election Therapy From My Basket of Deplorables

The election was a complete repudiation of Barack Obama: his fantasy world of political correctness, the politicization of the Justice Department and the I.R.S., an out-of-control E.P.A., his neutering of the military, his nonsupport of the police and his fixation on things like transgender bathrooms. Since he became president, his party has lost 63 House seats, 10 Senate seats and 14 governorships.

The country had signaled strongly in the last two midterms that they were not happy. The Dems' answer was to give them more of the same from a person they did not like or trust.

Preaching — and pandering — with a message of inclusion, the Democrats have instead become a party where incivility and bad manners are taken for granted, rudeness is routine, religion is mocked and there is absolutely no respect for a differing opinion. This did not go down well in the Midwest, where Trump flipped three blue states and 44 electoral votes.

The rudeness reached its peak when Vice President elect Mike Pence was booed by attendees of "Hamilton" and then pompously lectured by the cast. This may play well with the New York theater crowd but is considered boorish and unacceptable by those of us taught to respect the office of the president and vice president, if not the occupants.

Here is a short primer for the young protesters. If your preferred candidate loses, there is no need for mass hysteria, canceled midterms, safe spaces, crying rooms or group primal screams. You might understand this better if you had not received participation trophies, undeserved grades to protect your feelings or even if you had a proper understanding of civics. The Democrats are now crying that Hillary had more popular votes. That can be her participation trophy.

 If any of my sons had told me they were too distraught over a national election to take an exam, I would have brought them home the next day, fearful of the instruction they were receiving. Not one of the top 50 colleges mandate one semester of Western Civilization. Maybe they should rethink that.

Mr. Trump received over 62 million votes, not all of them cast by homophobes, Islamaphobes, racists, sexists, misogynists or any other "ists." I would caution Trump deniers that all of the crying and whining is not good preparation for the coming storm. The liberal media, both print and electronic, has lost all credibility. I am reasonably sure that none of the mainstream print media had stories prepared for a Trump victory. I watched the networks and cable stations in their midnight meltdown — embodied by Rachel Maddow explaining to viewers that they were not having a "terrible, terrible dream" and that they had not died and "gone to hell."

The media's criticism of Trump's high-level picks as "not diverse enough" or "too white and male" — a day before he named two women and offered a cabinet position to an African-American — magnified this fact.

Here is a final word to my Democratic friends. The election is over. There will not be a do-over. So let me bid farewell to Al Sharpton, Ben Rhodes and the Clintons. Note to Cher, Barbra, Amy Schumer and Lena Dunham: Your plane is waiting. And to Jon Stewart, who talked about moving to another planet: Your spaceship is waiting. To Bruce Springsteen, Jay Z, Beyoncé and Katy Perry, thanks for the free concerts. And finally, to all the foreign countries that contributed to the Clinton Foundation, there will not be a payoff or a rebate.

As Eddie Murphy so eloquently stated in the movie "48 Hours., "There's a new sheriff in town." And he is going to be here for 1,461 days. Merry Christmas.

Clear as mud

ARE you confused by what is going on in the Middle East? Let me explain.

We support the Iraqi government in the fight against Islamic State. We don't like IS, but IS is supported by Saudi Arabia, whom we do like.

We don't like President Assad in Syria. We support the fight against him, but not IS, which is also fighting against him.

We don't like Iran, but Iran supports the Iraqi government against IS. So, some of our friends support our enemies and some of our enemies are our friends, and some of our enemies are fighting against our other enemies, whom we want to lose, but we don't want our enemies who are fighting our enemies to win.

If the people we want to defeat are defeated, they might be replaced by people we like even less. And all this was started by us invading a country to drive out terrorists who weren't actually there until we went in to drive them out. Do you understand now?

AUBREY BAILEY, Fleet, Hants.

No Wonder Liberals are so confused

I used to think I was just a regular guy, but I was born white, which now, whether I like it or not, makes me a racist.

I am a fiscal and moral conservative, which by today's standards, makes me a fascist.

I am heterosexual, which according to gay folks, now makes me a homophobic.

I am non-union, which makes me a traitor to the working class and an ally of big business.

I am a Christian, which now labels me as an infidel.

I believe in the 2nd Amendment, which now makes me a member of the vast gun lobby.

I am older than 65, which makes me a useless old man.

I think and I reason, therefore I doubt much that the main stream media tells me, which must make me a reactionary.

I am proud of my heritage and our inclusive American culture, which makes me a xenophobe.

I value my safety and that of my family and I appreciate the police and the legal system, which makes me a right-wing extremist.

I believe in hard work, fair play, and fair compensation according to each individual's merits, which today makes me an anti-socialist.

I believe in the defense and protection of the homeland for and by all citizens, which now makes me a militant.

Now, a sick old woman is calling me and my friends a basket of deplorables.

Please help me come to terms with the new me, because I'm just not sure who I am anymore !

I would like to thank all my friends for sticking with me through these abrupt, new found changes in my life and my thinking!

I just can't imagine or understand what's happened to me so quickly !

Funny, it's all just taken place over the last 7 or 8 years ! I'm now afraid to go into either restroom!

The Difference Between Common Sense and Political Correctness

by Jeff Foxworthy

If plastic water bottles are okay, but plastic bags are banned, — you might live in a nation (state) that was founded by geniuses but is run by idiots. WE DO LIVE IN SUCH A DUMB COUNTRY!

If you can get arrested for hunting or fishing without a license, but not for entering and remaining in the country illegally — you might live in a nation that was founded by geniuses but is run by idiots.

If you have to get your parents' permission to go on a field trip or to take an aspirin in school, but not to get an abortion — you might live in a nation that was founded by geniuses but is run by idiots.

If you must show your identification to board an airplane, cash a check, buy liquor, or check out a library book and rent a video, but not to vote for who runs the government — you might live in a nation that was founded by geniuses but is run by idiots.

If the government wants to prevent stable, law-abiding citizens from owning gun magazines that hold more than ten rounds, but gives twenty F-16 fighter jets to the crazy new leaders in Egypt — you might live in a nation that was founded by geniuses but is run by idiots.

If, in the nation's largest city, you can buy two 16-ounce sodas, but not one 24-ounce soda, because 24 ounces of a sugary drink might make you fat — you might live in a nation that was founded by geniuses but is run by idiots.

If an 80-year-old woman who is confined to a wheelchair or a three-year-old girl can be strip-searched by the TSA at the airport, but a woman in a burka or a hijab is only subject to having her neck and head searched — you might live in a nation that was founded by geniuses but is run by idiots.

If your government believes that the best way to eradicate trillions of dollars of debt is to spend trillions more — you might live in a nation that was founded by geniuses but is run by idiots.

If a seven-year-old boy can be thrown out of school for saying his teacher is "cute" but hosting a sexual exploration or diversity class in grade school is perfectly acceptable — you might live in a nation that was founded by geniuses but is run by idiots.

If hard work and success are met with higher taxes and more government regulation and intrusion while not working is rewarded with Food Stamps, WIC checks, Medicaid benefits, subsidized housing, and free cell phones — you might live in a nation that was founded by geniuses but is run by idiots.

If you pay your mortgage faithfully, denying yourself the newest big-screen TV, while your neighbor buys iPhones, time shares, a wall-sized do-it-all plasma screen TV and new cars, and the government forgives his debt when he defaults on his mortgage — you might live in a nation that was founded by geniuses but is run by idiots.

If being stripped of your Constitutional right to defend yourself makes you more "safe" according to the government — you might live in a nation that was founded by geniuses but is run by idiots.

THINK BEFORE YOU VOTE IN ALL UPCOMING ELECTIONS. MOST OF THE IDIOTS RUNNING THIS COUNTRY SAY ONE THING AND DO THE OPPOSITE KNOWING THAT THE PEOPLE WHO VOTED THEM IN DO NOT PAY ATTENTION

LET'S SEE IF I GOT THIS RIGHT!

IF YOU CROSS THE NORTH KOREAN BORDER ILLEGALLY YOU GET 12 YEARS HARD LABOR.

IF YOU CROSS THE IRANIAN BORDER ILLEGALLY YOU ARE DETAINED INDEFINITELY.

IF YOU CROSS THE AFGHAN BORDER ILLEGALLY, YOU GET SHOT.

IF YOU CROSS THE SAUDI ARABIAN BORDER ILLEGALLY YOU WILL BE JAILED.

IF YOU CROSS THE CHINESE BORDER ILLEGALLY YOU MAY NEVER BE HEARD FROM AGAIN.

IF YOU CROSS THE VENEZUELAN BORDER ILLEGALLY YOU WILL BE BRANDED A SPY AND YOUR FATE WILL BE SEALED.

IF YOU CROSS THE CUBAN BORDER ILLEGALLY YOU WILL BE THROWN INTO POLITICAL PRISON TO ROT.

IF YOU CROSS THE U.S. BORDER ILLEGALLY YOU GET:

A JOB, A DRIVERS LICENSE, SOCIAL SECURITY CARD, WELFARE, FOOD STAMPS, CREDIT CARDS, SUBSIDIZED RENT OR A LOAN TO BUY A HOUSE, FREE EDUCATION, FREE HEALTH CARE, A LOBBYIST IN WASHINGTON, BILLIONS OF DOLLARS WORTH OF PUBLIC DOCUMENTS PRINTED IN YOUR LANGUAGE, THE RIGHT TO CARRY YOUR COUNTRY'S FLAG WHILE YOU PROTEST THAT YOU DON'T GET ENOUGH RESPECT, AND, IN MANY INSTANCES, YOU CAN VOTE.

I JUST WANTED TO MAKE SURE I HAD A FIRM GRASP ON THE SITUATION!

A POLITICAL JOKE

I told my son, "You will marry the girl I choose."
He said, "No."
I told him, "She is Bill Gate's daughter."
He said, "Yes."

I called Bill Gates and said, "I want your daughter to marry my son."
Bill Gates said, "No."
I told Bill Gates, "My son is the CEO of World Bank."
Bill Gates said, "Okay."

I called the president of World Bank and asked him to make my son the CEO.
He said, "No."
I told him, "My son is Bill Gate's son-in-law."
He said, "Okay."

And this is how politics works!

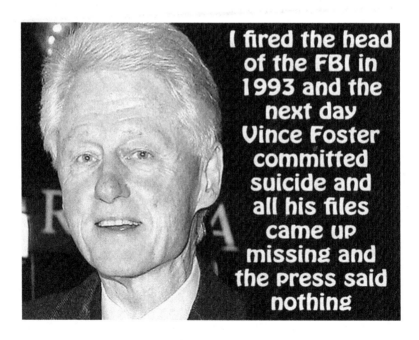

I fired the head of the FBI in 1993 and the next day Vince Foster committed suicide and all his files came up missing and the press said nothing

SIMPLY GENIUS

I took down my Rebel flag (which you can't buy on Ebay anymore) and peeled the NRA sticker off my front window. I disconnected my home alarm system and quit the Neighborhood Watch. I bought two Pakistani flags and put one at each corner of the front yard. Then I purchased the black flag of ISIS (which you CAN Buy on Ebay) and ran it up the flag pole.

Now the local police, sheriff, FBI, CIA, NSA, Homeland Security, Secret Service and other agencies are all watching my house 24/7. I've NEVER felt safer and I'm saving $69.95 a month that ADT security used to charge me.

Plus, I bought burkas for me to wear when I shop or travel. Everyone moves out of the way, and security can't pat me down. If they say I'm a male wearing a burka, I just say I'm feeling like a woman today.

Safe at last.

Mike

DAILY ▊ NEWS

Friday, November 4, 1949   Tel. MUrray Hill 2-1234

Published daily except Sunday by News Syndicate Co., Inc., 220 E. 42d St. Borough of Manhattan, New York 17, N. Y. Daily mail subscription rates: U. S., $15.00. Canada, $15.00 a year. For the Daily and Sunday News, U. S., $20.00 per year; Canada, $22.50. President and general manager, F. M. Flynn; executive editor and secretary, Richard W. Clarke.

MEMBER OF THE ASSOCIATED PRESS

The Associated Press is entitled exclusively to the use for republication of all the local news printed in this newspaper, as well as all AP news dispatches.

ODE TO THE WELFARE STATE

Mr. Truman's St. Paul, Minn., pie-for-everybody speech last night reminded us that, at the tail-end of the recent session of Congress, Representative Clarence J. Brown (R-Ohio) jammed into the Congressional Record the following poem, describing its author only as "a prominent Democrat of the State of Georgia":

DEMOCRATIC DIALOG

Father, must I go to work?
  No, my lucky son.
We're living now on Easy Street
  On dough from Washington.

We've left it up to Uncle Sam,
  So don't get exercised.
Nobody has to give a damn—
  We've all been subsidized.

But if Sam treats us all so well
  And feeds us milk and honey,
Please, daddy, tell me what the hell
  He's going to use for money.

Don't worry, bub, there's not a hitch
  In this here noble plan—
He simply soaks the filthy rich
  And helps the common man.

But, father, won't there come a time
  When they run out of cash
And we have left them not a dime
  When things will go to smash?

My faith in you is shrinking, son,
  You nosy little brat;
You do too damn much thinking, son,
  To be a Democrat.

CHARLIE REESE'S FINAL COLUMN A GREAT READ!

A very interesting column. COMPLETELY NEUTRAL. Be sure to read the poem at the end. Charley Reese's final column for the Orlando Sentinel. He has been a journalist for 49 years. He is retiring and this is HIS LAST COLUMN. Be sure to read the Tax List at the end.

This is about as clear and easy to understand as it can be. The article below is completely neutral, neither anti-republican nor democrat. Charlie Reese, a retired reporter for the Orlando Sentinel, has hit the nail directly on the head, defining clearly who it is that in the final analysis must assume responsibility for the judgments made that impact each one of us every day. It's a relatively short but good read. Worth the time. Worth remembering!

545 vs. 300,000,000 People- by Charlie Reese

Politicians are the only people in the world who create problems and then campaign against them.

Have you ever wondered, if both the Democrats and the Republicans are against deficits, WHY do we have deficits?

Have you ever wondered, if all the politicians are against inflation and high taxes, WHY do we have inflation and high taxes?

You and I don't propose a federal budget. The President does. You and I don't have the Constitutional authority to vote on appropriations. The House of Representatives does.

You and I don't write the tax code, Congress does. You and I don't set fiscal policy, Congress does.

You and I don't control monetary policy, the Federal Reserve Bank does.

One hundred senators, 435 congressmen, one President, and nine Supreme Court justices equates to 545 human beings out of the 300 million are directly, legally, morally, and individually responsible for the domestic problems that plague this country.

I excluded the members of the Federal Reserve Board because that problem was created by the Congress. In 1913, Congress delegated its Constitutional duty to provide a sound currency to a federally chartered, but private, central bank.

I excluded all the special interests and lobbyists for a sound reason. They have no legal authority. They have no ability to coerce a Senator, a Congressman, or a President to do one cotton-picking thing. I don't care if they offer a politician $1 million dollars in cash.

The politician has the power to accept or reject it. No matter what the lobbyist promises, it is the legislator's responsibility to determine how he votes.

Those 545 human beings spend much of their energy convincing you that what they did is not their fault. They cooperate in this common con regardless of party.

What separates a politician from a normal human being is an excessive amount of gall. No normal human being would have the gall of a Speaker, who stood up and criticized the President for creating deficits. The President can only propose a budget. He cannot force the Congress to accept it.

The Constitution, which is the supreme law of the land, gives sole responsibility to the House of Representatives for originating and approving appropriations and taxes.

Who is the speaker of the House now? He is the leader of the majority party. He and fellow House members, not the President, can approve any budget they want. If the President vetoes it, they can pass it over his veto if they agree to.

It seems inconceivable to me that a nation of 300 million cannot replace 545 people who stand convicted -- by present facts -- of incompetence and irresponsibility. I can't think of a single domestic problem that is not traceable directly to those 545 people. When you fully grasp the plain truth that 545 people exercise the power of the Federal Government, then it must follow that what exists is what they want to exist.

If the tax code is unfair, it's because they want it unfair. If the budget is in the red, it's because they want it in the red.

If the Army & Marines are in Iraq and Afghanistan it's because they want them in Iraq and Afghanistan. If they do not receive social security but are on an elite retirement plan not available to the people, it's because they want it that way.

There are no insoluble government problems.

Do not let these 545 people shift the blame to bureaucrats, whom they hire and whose jobs they can abolish; to lobbyists, whose gifts and advice they can reject; to regulators, to whom they give the power to regulate and from whom they can take this power.

Above all, do not let them con you into the belief that there exists disembodied mystical forces like "the economy," "inflation," or "politics" that prevent them from doing what they take an oath to do.

Those 545 people, and they alone, are responsible. They, and they alone, have the power. They and they alone, should be held accountable by the people who are their bosses, provided the voters have the gumption to manage their own employees.

We should vote all of them out of office and clean up their mess!

What you do with this article now that you have read it... is up to you.

This might be funny if it weren't so true.

Be sure to read all the way to the end:
Tax his land,
Tax his bed,
Tax the table, at which he's fed.
Tax his tractor,
Tax his mule,
Teach him taxes are the rule.
Tax his work,
Tax his pay, he works for peanuts anyway!
Tax his cow,
Tax his goat,
Tax his pants,
Tax his coat.
Tax his ties,

Tax his shirt,
Tax his work,
Tax his dirt.
Tax his tobacco,
Tax his drink,
Tax him if he tries to think.
Tax his cigars,
Tax his beers,
If he cries tax his tears.
Tax his car,
Tax his gas,
Find other ways to tax his ass.
Tax all he has, then let him know that you won't be done till he has no dough.
When he screams and hollers; then tax him some more, tax him till he's good and sore.
Then tax his coffin,
Tax his grave,
Tax the sod into which he's laid...
Put these words upon his tomb,
"Taxes drove me to my doom..."
When he's gone, do not relax,
it's time to apply, the Inheritance tax.

Accounts Receivable Tax
Building Permit Tax
CDL license Tax
Cigarette Tax
Corporate Income Tax
Dog License Tax
Excise Taxes

Federal Income Tax
Federal Unemployment Tax (FUTA)
Fishing License Tax
Food License Tax
Fuel Permit Tax
Gasoline Tax (currently 44.75 cents per gallon)
Gross Receipts Tax
Hunting License Tax
Inheritance Tax
Inventory Tax
IRS Interest Charges IRS Penalties (tax on top of tax)
Liquor Tax
Luxury Taxes
Marriage License Tax
Medicare Tax
Personal Property Tax
Property Tax
Real Estate Tax
Service Charge Tax
Social Security Tax
Road Usage Tax
Recreational Vehicle Tax
Sales Tax
School Tax
State Income Tax
State Unemployment Tax (SUTA)
Telephone Federal Excise Tax
Telephone Federal Universal Service Fee Tax
Telephone Federal, State and Local Surcharge Taxes

Telephone Minimum Usage Surcharge Tax
Telephone Recurring and Nonrecurring Charges
Tax
Telephone State and Local Tax
Telephone Usage Charge Tax
Utility Taxes
Vehicle License Registration Tax
Vehicle Sales Tax
Watercraft Registration Tax
Well Permit Tax
Workers Compensation Tax

STILL THINK THIS IS FUNNY?

Not one of these taxes existed 100 years ago, and our nation was the most prosperous in the world.

We had absolutely no national debt, had the largest middle class in the world, and Mom, if greed, stayed home to raise the kids.

What in the heck happened? Can you spell "politicians?"

What has America become?

Editor,

Has America become the land of the special interest and home of the double standard?

Let's see: if we lie to the Congress, it's a felony and if the congress lies to us its just politics; if we dislike a black person, we're racist and if a black dislikes whites, it's their 1st Amendment right; the government spends millions to rehabilitate criminals and they do almost nothing for the victims; in public schools you can teach that homosexuality is OK, but you better not use the word God in an unborn process; you can kill an unborn child, but its wrong to execute a mass murderer; we don't burn books in America, we now rewrite them; we got rid of the communist and socialist threat by renaming them progressives; we are unable to close our border with Mexico, but have no problem protecting the 38th parallel in Korea; if you protest against President Obama's policies you're a terrorist, but if you burned an American flag or George Bush in effigy it was your 1st Amendment right.

You can have pornography on TV or the internet, but you better not put a nativity scene in a public park during Christmas; we have eliminated all criminals in America, they are now called sick people; we can use a human fetus for medical research, but it's wrong to use an animal.

We take money from those who work hard for it and give it to those who don't want to work; we all support the Constitution, but only when it supports our political ideology; we still have freedom of speech, but only if we are being politically correct; parenting has been replaced with Ritalin and video games; the land of opportunity is now the land of hand outs; the similarity between Hurricane Katrina and the gulf oil spill is that neither president did anything to help.

And how do we handle a major crisis today? The government appoints a committee to determine who's at fault, then threatens them, passes a law, raises our taxes; tells us the problem is solved so they can get back to their reelection campaign.

What has happened to the land of the free and home of the brave?

— Ken Huber
Tawas City

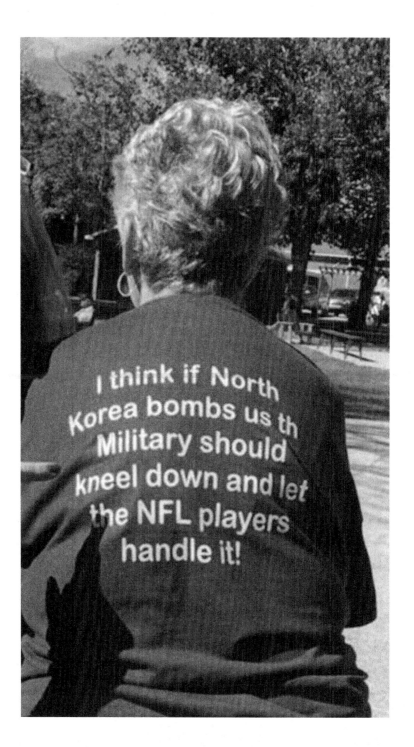

RAISE YOUR HAND IF YOU'RE UNDER A CRIMINAL INVESTIGATION.

Final Thoughts

The Last Entry for Jan and Dahk's Scrapbook 2017

This is our 15th and last Scrapbook. We don't know where the years have gone, but such speed seems to be normal; it appears to go faster with each passing year. Jan and I hope that you have kept our yearly issues of this Scrapbook, so now you'll have the full set. We would not like to think that all of our books have been trashed or thrown out over the past 15 years, but treasured and retained, as our family has felt about them.

It has been enjoyable doing the books, but now we are at that age where keeping up with the work to be done, i.e., saving and accumulating materials, weeding out and adding to the content, editing, finding pictures and so forth has become a bit laborious for us older folks, rather than fun like it used to be. We don't want our Scrapbooks to become a chore, but it has become more arduous for Jan and me to do. We do hope you have been as entertained and informed by our Scrapbooks since 2003, as we have felt joyous in writing and publishing them.

We have also weaned down our publishing efforts for other authors' books with Black Forest Press and the Tennessee Publishing House. This has been our 26th year of book publishing. Over that stretch of time, we have, in total, published over 2,000 books by over 900 different authors. Some authors have done multiple books with us like our dear deceased author and friend Scott Beemer. Scott did 26 books with us. God rest his soul. He wrote up until his passing last year. Scott was 96 years old and a fine Christian man. We've had many fine authors who have written numerous excellent books which we have enjoyed publishing. Scotty was the most prolific and God-centered.

However, the time has now come for our retirement and redirecting and targeting our hours for doing a godly plan of Christian work. Nonetheless, we will continue to write our Covenant Christian Bible Informational booklets, which we give freely to those interested in coming to Jesus Christ and beginning either a new relationship with Him, or strengthening an older relationship with Him. We do hope you have encouraging thoughts for us doing the Lord's work, and we ask for your prayers for a successful ministry for Christ.

If you care to have any of our booklets, which are all about 20 pages long and 5 ½ by 8 ½ in size, let us know by emailing me (Dahk) at my desk: dahkknox@embarqmail.com. A list of our booklets follows. Our mailing address is: Drs. Dahk & Jan Knox, Covenant Christian Ministries, Inc., 488 Mountain View Drive, Mosheim, TN 37818-3524.

We are a 501c3 tax exempt, non-profit Christian corporation in the State of Tennessee. Any donations or contributions for printing and postage expenses is tax deductible and much appreciated. This is especially helpful for large orders. Our Ministry is now ten years old.

Jan is being compelled to spend all this extra time doing more machine embroidery! (hmmmmmmmm, go figure!) She loves doing it, and typically ends up giving lots of it away as a means for a ministry. The joy she gets in this creativity is boundless. So, Jan. . . carry on!

God bless y'all and do keep in touch with us down here in the holler at Belle Arden Run.

Our love and best wishes. Dahk and Jan Knox

Singing: "Happy trails to you, until we meet again."

It's been a great 35 plus years and still counting. Praise the
Lord for all of His many blessings.

CPSIA information can be obtained
at www.ICGtesting.com
Printed in the USA
LVOW13s0637241117
557256LV00002BA/2/P